# THE MAZE

## HER RUDE AWAKENING

Lauren Brunell,

Thank you for your

support, I hope

you enjoy this

story!

Alexandra Russell

## PINA PUBLISHING ё SEATTLE

For information about special discounts for bulk purchases contact:
sales@pinapublishing.com

Manufactured in the United States of America
Library of Congress Cataloging-in-Publication Data Russell, Alexandra.

Summary:
The awakening process is nothing less than terrifying. After years of numbing, suppressing, and running from her problems, Pearl Cassel finds herself lost in the outskirts of her mind, slowly being eaten alive by her crippling depression and suicidal thoughts. Driven into danger by the darkness within, Pearl suddenly gets abducted by a deranged hypnotherapist who puts her under into this place known as *The Maze*. However, this Maze is unlike any other maze. *The Maze* takes place within the mind, carving through the darkest parts of her psyche, leading her to nothing but the most cruel, horrific obstacles she could face. Pearl is forced to face her demons, yet one can only take so much. To escape *The Maze*, she must peel back her layers, feel the deaths of her ego, and ultimately, unravel her truth within. Will Pearl find her way out of *The Maze* alive? Or will she be forever trapped in her hellish mind with the rest of the victims of depression? Are you willing to dive into the darkness that many are too scared to face? Join Pearl on her journey through *The Maze* to find out.

ISBN:
978-1-943493-51-7 (paperback)
978-1-943493-49-4 (ebook)
978-1-943493-50-0 (hardcover)

[1. Thriller. 2. Psychological. 3. Self-Help. 4. Horror. 5. Adventure. 6. Adult. 7. Young Adult. 8. Education]

Dedicated to my Dad.
Rest in Paradise.
Until we meet again.

To my Mom and Neil.
Thank you for your endless love and support.

To Nick.
Thank you for everything.

To Amanda and Alyssa.
My best friends.

To Mimi.
Thank you for your guidance.

To Choury.
Thank you for sharing your light during my darkest of times.

To the rest of my family and friends.
I am grateful for everyone in my life.

And most importantly—
To anyone who is or has struggled with depression.
You are not alone.
For this moment is only temporary.

May this story be more than just a scary one.

♥

A note from the author—
This story, despite painting hypnosis in a negative light, is in no way a reflection of the sentiments of the practice, which can be very beneficial to many, including myself.

Now, let's get on with the story.

Based on a nightmare, personal experience,
& a dark imagination.

# TABLE OF CONTENTS

# PSYCH WARD

1

"Here we are." The nurse welcomed the film crew into a long, narrow hallway. A crisp chill lingered throughout, and the lights overhead flickered slightly, barely lighting the path ahead. Multiple steel doors, all triple locked, stood tall before them, and taped along the walls hung dozens of dull, lifeless paintings, most of which appeared to bring more sadness than joy. One painting displayed a blue vase with a bouquet of wilted sunflowers, while another depicted a grey lake lying below a purple mountain range, with a washed-out sun setting behind. The three men followed the nurse out of the elevator with their stomachs lodged up into their throats. Tom, the interviewer, followed by the cameraman, Allan, and the sound mixer, Randy, skulked forward, observing their new surroundings.

"Is it always this eerie around here?" Allan asked nervously under his breath.

"Welcome to Everred Psychiatric Asylum," the nurse replied. "There's a reason we are one of the most famous, yet dangerous mental hospitals in the country. Some days are quieter than others, but of course it just depends on the mood of our patients. Some patients are more calm and stable, while others can be a bit more bloody-minded. You know, the ones that are kicking, screaming, fighting, and so forth. Just last week, we had a patient check in who believed a swarm of bees was flying around inside his head. He ended up clawing his own scalp, hoping he would stop 'the bees.' Then, he found his way here, drenched in his own blood. It took four male nurses to keep him from digging any deeper."

"Wow, really?" Randy responded, hardly believing it.

"Why so shocked?" Tom asked Randy.

"I mean, I don't know. I guess I'm not."

"I'm sure you can tell a lot more interesting stories from working here," Allan interrupted his colleagues, still interested in the woman's tale. "It's all part of the territory," she replied. "The patients that are admitted to Everred are either dangerously depressed, dangerously deranged, or both. Many of these patients don't deserve to be here. They suffer so deeply, so severely, that they have basically become slaves to their own minds. It's sad, really. But the other patients, on the other hand, the ones with unholy, disturbing crimes underneath their belts, deserve nothing less than being here. I'll tell you what, I never have a boring day at work."

"Must be draining though sometimes, wouldn't you say?" Tom asked.

"Well, sure. But like I said, it comes with the territory." She continued to lead them closer toward room 515.

Randy cleared his throat. "So, why aren't there many people on this floor?"

"We keep all of our highly unstable and dangerous patients on this floor. You know, people like Doc Stephens. However, his room is at the very end of the hall, away from everyone else. The power that man possesses is like no other. It is extremely important for him to be excluded from the outside world. He has darker shadows than any other person I have ever seen come through this place. I am surprised you gentlemen are willingly here to see him," the nurse stated firmly, as she continued to guide them further down the hall. The three men glanced over at one another with worried, yet determined eyes. Within a few more steps, door 515 became clear in sight. "This is it."

The four of them approached a massive, steel door, securely locked with two deadbolts and one padlock. The nurse unlocked the deadbolts first, then slid the key into the padlock, yet before she turned the tumblers, she paused for a moment, glancing over her shoulder toward the film crew. "Remember, do not look into his eyes. I cannot stress this enough to you," she urged, with worry in her own eyes.

"We understand," Tom responded, while Allan and Randy nodded their heads in agreement.

"And you have nothing sharp on you, right?"

"Nope, we've already been searched for anything sharp or stringy."

The nurse nodded, looked back toward the door, and unlocked the last lock. The three men gulped behind her.

She pulled the door open wide. The film crew, without thinking, held their breath with anticipation as they walked through the door. Not only were they beyond anxious to see him, but to speak to one of the world's most malevolent people in human history felt simply breathtaking, in the most fascinating, yet horrifying way. The door shut behind them on its own.

2

They walked through another narrow hallway that led them into a bright, bare room. Inside, there was a bed with an old comforter, a couple of lounge chairs, and a small, metal side table. On the side table sat psychology, hypnosis, and spiritual awakening textbooks stacked high on top of one another. Next to the stack of books rested a doctorate degree for psychology, a hypnotherapy certification, a few other doctorates all awarded to Stephens, and a few sheets of paper with nothing but pen marks scratched all over them. Tom, Allan, and Randy examined the space with unease and fascination.

"Doc, you have some visitors today. Remember we told you they were coming?" The nurse asked. The man sat on the edge of his bed with his back facing the door, until suddenly, he shot a glance over his shoulder and jumped quickly onto his feet. The crew returned the glance, bracing themselves for who they have anticipated seeing for so long; Doctor Doc L. Stephens, one of the most fearsome humans to have ever walked the earth.

Stephens looked younger than his reported old age. He had a long, narrow face and bright, rejuvenated skin. He had crow's feet living beside his eyes and wrinkles indented into his cheeks, revealing years of wide, devious smiles. The little hair he had growing on his head carried a greyish-brown hue and appeared shaggy and unkempt. He wore a white, long sleeve shirt and white pants provided by the hospital, while his feet remained bare. But the one thing that caught the men's attention the most were Doc's hypnotizing, deceitful eyes. His eyes pierced with a yellowish blue tone, and although they shined brightly, they illuminated an essence of mysterious darkness. Stephens had been sweeping the nation with his horrific stories of mind-control and essentially, mass murder. He was known all over the globe for his wicked power, and for the unfortunate stories of his crucifixion victims. He was an evil genius, and the film crew felt more than nervous to interview him. The men looked away from Doc's eyes as they made their way further into the room.

"Ah, yes! Ha! Welcome to my office, fellas! I have been looking forward to this since the moment I heard you were coming." Doc stared at Tom, Allan, and Randy with a wide smile painted across his face.

"Hello Doctor, my name is Tom, I'll be conducting your interview today," Tom introduced himself, keeping his eyes glued to Doc's forehead. "This is Randy, our sound mixer, and Allan, our cameraman. We work for Flixview."

Doc laughed out loud. "Flixview, huh? Is that what they are calling it now?"

"It is just another streaming platform that allows you to watch movies and television shows online. Thank you for taking time out of your day to talk to us."

"Oh, of course!" Doc smiled, reaching his hand out for a shake.

Hesitant, Tom reached his hand forward and grabbed hold of Doc's. Doc's grip felt firm, a bit painful, even.

"Let's get to it! Shall we?" Doc exclaimed.

While the crew began to set up their equipment, the nurse called in security for backup. Within roughly five seconds, two tall, wide men, both constructed of nothing more than pure muscle, stampeded through the steel door frame. Each of them carried an M1911 on their hip, loaded and ready to fire. One of the security guards stood behind the crew, while the other stood closer to Doc. Meanwhile, Doc sat tall at the end of his bed. His shoulders rolled down his spine, his chin rose slightly up toward the ceiling, and his hands rested interlaced on his lap. His breath flowed voluntarily slowly, and he had a soft, crooked smile slithering from ear to ear. He seemed more than comfortable and ready for the camera, as if he had been awaiting this moment, too.

After a few short minutes, they had everything ready and set in position. Allan stood behind the camera while Randy hovered the mic over Doc's head.

"You guys ready?" Tom asked his crew, taking a seat next to Doc. Allan and Randy both returned a subtle nod. "Alright, here we go."

"Three, two," Allan pointed his finger and mouthed the word 'one' to Tom and Doc, giving them the green light to go.


3


Despite the fifteen years that Tom had been interviewing people around the world, many inspiring and many terrifying, he had never felt more nervous than he did sitting in the same room as Dr. Doc Stephens. Tom focused on Doc's forehead, licked his chapped lips, and began to speak.

"Ca—can you start by telling us who you are?" He stuttered anxiously.

"I am Doctor Doc Lance Stephens. I am a certified doctor, psychologist, and hypnotherapist. However, hypnotherapy is my specialty. At least, that is where I gain the most pleasure from. I have been practicing hypnosis for about fifty years and counting." He spoke clearly and confidently.

"How old are you?"

"I am seventy-nine years old."

"You said hypnotherapy is your specialty. What kind of patients did you have coming to see you?"

"Mostly patients that were experiencing severe depression and suicidal thoughts. People who had a difficult time seeing the light within the dark."

"How did they find you?" Tom asked, chipping away at his own fingers.

Doc paused for a moment and thought to himself. Then, he responded with a crack in his voice. "Some found me, and for the others... I guess you could say that I found them."

"Wha—what exactly did your sessions with them en—entail?"

"I specialized in rewiring the brain from the inside out."

"Can you tell us a little more about that?" Tom questioned.

Doc's smile grew even wider. "I presented my patients with an opportunity to step into their subconscious mind, ultimately to shift their perspective."

"Shift their perspective?"

"Of course," Doc said, surprised. "Similar to someone taking a hit of LSD or undergoing a year-long meditation, it is something so small, yet so powerful. It is strong enough to change an entire human's outlook and ultimately, their entire life. I mean, this is a human life we are talking about!" Doc's voice grew louder and his energy more eager. He flailed his hands in the air and rocked back and forth on the bed.

Tom shifted his gaze down and kept his head low, making sure his eyes never met Doc's. He skimmed down his list of questions, keeping his shoulders raised toward his ears.

"If you had the option to make your life the best it could be, wouldn't you go for it?" Doc continued.

Tom looked toward Doc with one eyebrow raised. "Why are you in an insane asylum, Doctor? What brought you here?"

"Ha, ha, ha," Doc snorted. He slapped his knees, took in a rich breath, and exhaled like a lion. "Apparently, according to the world, my mind is too powerful for the public. I might as well be Einstein or something. Idolized by many. Everyone knows about me." A smile crept across his face once again.

All three men of Flixview glanced toward one another doubtfully.

"Why are you so confident?" Tom continued, gulping back his anxiety while taking the risk. He managed to look past him, restricting his eyes from meeting Doc's. Meanwhile, both security guards brought their hands to their hips, anticipating the mastermind's next move. Doc quickly grew agitated with Tom's presence and his twisted smile faded into a scowl. His voice grew low and he spoke slowly, as he pierced his devilish eyes through Tom's.

"I am not a murderer, like the world thinks I am. All I have ever wanted to do is help those who are suffering. It is a shame that the world sees me as this evil monster. When really, I am not the one that ended the lives of those who have come to see me." His eyes began to morph black with rage and his skin speckled red. "I was the bridge that connected their pathetic minds to their highest of psyche. I was the guide that revealed simply what they felt every single day. This place of darkness was a place they brought themselves to all on their own; all I did was bring them face to face with their shadows that hid within them. Unfortunately, many of them simply could not handle it."

"According to records, a total of one hundred fifty-seven patients were reported to never wake up after attending a hypnotherapy session with you. Is this true?"

Doc guffawed at Tom as his eyes rolled into the back of his skull. "I thought this was going to be a fun interview."

"Is this true, Doc?"

He paused for a moment. "Not sure. Hard to keep track of so many patients. What's your point?"

"My point is that you seem to be extremely confident for someone who has an unholy amount of homicide charges against them, and I am wondering why." The room grew even more tense. Tom fell silent, anticipating Doc's answer. Doc finally complied.

"I can't help that those people can't control the power of their own minds."

"But you did essentially take over their minds, did you not? You forced them to enter a state of consciousness that they had no chance of escaping from. They were powerless, because of you. They became a sack of lifeless flesh, yet a forever-existing soul floating in a dimension of trapped consciousness. Do you believe they wanted that?"

Doc furrowed his brows. "Like I said, I granted them access. It was up to them to find their way out."

"Find their way out of where?"

Doc's warped smile crept across his face once again. "The Maze." He paused for a moment, laughing to himself. "The Maze within their mind."

# Twenty Years Ago

1

She walked through the front door with her gaze shifted down. Her hands dug deep into her pockets and she kept her chin slightly tucked toward her chest. Her breath flowed short, and the nerves in her stomach began to tighten. Making her way toward the staircase, she headed up to the second floor and down another long, endless hallway, gripping the straps of her backpack tightly in her fists. With anticipation, the young woman took one step after another, breathing anxiously and involuntarily. Eventually, she arrived at her destination. She approached a door that stood underneath a large sign, reading "Psychiatry, Waiting Room One." She pulled open the heavy, grey door, shambled herself into the waiting room, and moseyed her way toward the front desk.

"Hey Pearl, how are you doing this week?" The receptionist greeted Pearl with a soft smile. The woman sat up tall with a gleaming demeanor, and she had short, silky, brunette curls that sat comfortably on her shoulders. She wore rectangular-shaped, brown glasses that rested low on the bridge of her nose, one lens more scratched than the other, and around her neck hung bright, pink pearls. Her red lips shined under the gloss, and her snow-white skin glowed bright.

"Hey Melinda. I'm still living, so that's something."

"Are you staying warm out there?" The receptionist asked her, changing the subject.

"I'm doing my best." Pearl responded, looking down at the floor.

Meanwhile, Melinda handed Pearl a clipboard with a questionnaire and pen attached.

"Alright, here you go sweetheart."

"Thanks." Pearl grabbed the clipboard and slipped a light smile toward the woman. She made her way to the furthest empty chair from every other person waiting. With her chin still tucked into her chest and her eyes glued on the floor, she shuffled her feet toward the cold, leather chair. Pearl sat quietly, fidgeting her way to comfort. She released her backpack and reusable water bottle on the chair next to her, and set the clipboard on her lap. Finally, she felt settled. Once she found comfort, she lifted her head and observed those around her.

Five people waited amongst Pearl. First, she noticed an old man sitting by himself. His skin drooped down his face and his cheeks were spotted with red. He had little to no eyebrows, and his hair was thinning not only on his face, but on the top of his head, too. He wore big, bulky glasses that sat low on his nose, and his jaw hung heavily. He wore a loose, cotton sweater vest that had big, black buttons lined up the front, and brown khakis that hovered barely over his dress shoes. His body sat like a statue, yet his mind wandered into oblivion as he stared at the wall in front of him.

Next, she noticed a woman, late thirties, also sitting far away from any other person in the room. Her brown hair was tied back into a messy bun and her eyelashes went out for a mile. She had olive brown skin, and the hair on her arms stuck up toward the ceiling. She breathed rapidly, while she bit her nails down to the nub. She, too, was filling out the same questionnaire that Pearl had on her lap.

The next person sat directly in the middle of the room, facing a flat screen television that was mounted along the back wall. He appeared to be around Pearl's age; early twenties. He had brown, shiny hair and crazed, blue eyes. He laughed uncomfortably loudly at the cartoons that flashed on the television screen, while rocking back and forth in his seat. He also had a clipboard that sat next to him, untouched, on a small, wooden side table.

The other two in the room looked to be a mother and son. The woman had long, blonde hair that was braided down her back. Her eyes carried big, dark circles underneath them, and her energy appeared to be noticeably drained. She seemed exhausted, as she took a big sigh in, and an even bigger sigh out. The woman kept her tired eyes locked down on her smartphone while her son sat deeply zoned into the cartoon trance. Her son, around age four or five, had shaggy, blonde hair and two large dimples that indented both sides of his face. He sat quietly, as his hypnotized eyes glistened up at the television screen. Suddenly, a back door swung open. A short, slim woman with a smile stretching from cheek to cheek entered the room.

"Daniel?" The woman politely asked the room.

The young man who sat laughing to himself jumped up and out of his seat, briskly spun around, and trotted toward the woman. She held the door open for him.

"Hello, Daniel! So nice to see you again today. How is your day going so far?"

The young man took a deep breath in, then exclaimed, "Hello there! Oh, my day is going fine! Tha—thank you for asking." The door slowly closed behind them and their voices slowly faded away.

Pearl shifted her gaze back down at the questionnaire, refocusing her attention back on herself. She put pen to paper and worked her way down the questions. Each question had an answer box that contained a number scale from one to four, one being not at all, and four being often, at least every day. Some of the questions included:

1. In the last week, how often have you experienced anxiety or negative thoughts that make you feel down, hopeless, or depressed?
   Pearl circled the number four.

2. In the last week, how often have you had thoughts of harming yourself?
   Pearl circled the number four.

3. In the last week, how often do you have thoughts that you are

worthless, a burden on others, and would be better off dead?

Pearl circled the number four.

4. In the last week, how often have you used a drug or prescription drug for non-medicinal purposes?

    She hesitated, this time, as she referred to the last week of her life. Then, she circled the number three.

5. In the last week, how many beverages containing at least two ounces of alcohol have you consumed?

    Pearl thought for a moment again, until she circled the number three.

The list went on for about fifteen more questions, each asking about her mental health, how she has been feeling, and what she has been doing. She responded to each of them accordingly, not thinking too hard about her responses. It was not her first time around the merry-go-round, and it sure as hell would not be her last, she believed. She knew this place like the back of her hand. However, for her to rewind her memories from the last week simply exhausted her. Frankly, it was quite difficult for her to recall the last week. Every day felt like a blur to Pearl. She found it challenging to remain present in the present moment when every moment she lived felt like hell. She believed that this moment, and every moment of her life, had been nothing worth living for. She felt unhappy, and she convinced herself that nobody else could ever understand the pain she felt festering within. *Why is this happening to me? Why can I never get a break? Why am I even here? What did I do to deserve everything I have gone through? We are all going to die anyway, so what is the point?* These questions constantly attacked her. She could not understand the point of living when she barely felt like she was living at all. Pearl was a victim of her own reality.

After Pearl finished her questionnaire, she grabbed her belongings, stood quietly up and out of her seat, and made her way back over to the front desk.

"Here you go," Pearl said as she returned the clipboard and pen back to Melinda.

"Thank you," the receptionist responded with a pleasant smile. "Michael will meet you in waiting room two today, okay? Have a good rest of your day, honey. See you next week."

"Sounds good. See you then." Pearl returned a fake smile, turned her body around, and made her way back out the front door and toward waiting room two, down the hall.

2

*Ah, waiting room two,* Pearl thought to herself. She dragged her feet and moved sluggishly. Exhaling a long sigh, she made her way toward the next door, opened it wide, and dragged her body inside.

Here, only one other single woman sat anxiously amongst the dozen empty chairs. The girl glanced up quick to see who had joined her, noticed Pearl, then instantly shifted her gaze back down. She looked like skin and bones. The girl had short and exceedingly thin auburn red hair that was straight as an arrow. She had crystal blue eyes that glistened underneath her flooded tears, and pasty, white skin. Her cheeks sunk into the sides of her face, and her teeth gnawed on her painted black nails. Her breath flew by, rapidly in and out of her lungs, but she did an excellent job at keeping it quiet. She appeared noticeably cold, as she continuously shivered underneath her large, navy blue sweater.

Pearl made her way to one of the empty chairs. She sat down, keeping her belongings on her lap this time. When she had settled down into this new space, she periodically glanced over at the sad girl. Pearl wondered the reason as to why she sat in the same room as she did. She thought about each tear that fell from her face and the reason for their fall. Pearl's heart felt pain for this human, as she could clearly see she was hurting, just like she was. Pearl wanted to tell her that it would all be okay, but she did not want to feed her lies. She, too, believed it would never be okay. There they sat, suffering in silence, holding space with one another, lost in the outskirts of their own minds.

About five minutes passed until another door in the room opened. The girl stood to her feet and walked through the open door, very quietly. The door closed behind her, and silence swept over the room.

In between the hushed walls, Pearl sat alone, stuck with only the thoughts that chattered through her mind. She reflected on her own life, her own journey, and her own misery. She wallowed in her own self-pity because she was convinced that the world had stuck a big, red target on her back. She constantly wondered what she did to deserve what she was going through, and why she still could not find happiness after the countless sessions she had with Michael. Pearl pondered why she was still coming to this place, and why nobody outside of her could solve all her problems. She believed that she would never find happiness as the craving to die grew hungrier than the craving to continue living. One thought after another, and another. She could not keep up. A shot of adrenaline released throughout her body, and she could physically feel her insides cooking like an oven. Sweat submerged from her temples and dripped down, while the pigmentation of her face morphed. She noticed the rhythm of her heart and how it just about beat entirely out of her chest. Anxiety crept throughout her being, the nerves inside her body constricted, and her stomach churned with nausea. Her mind could not think of anything but the feeling of anxiety taking control of her once again. A single tear rolled down her flushed cheeks, when suddenly, the door opened. Michael stood in the doorway, smiling at Pearl.

Pearl sat up, upholding a strong persona, as if zero darkness clouded her mind. However, on the inside, she screamed at the top of her lungs. She picked up her belongings, faltered to the door, and followed Michael down the hall into another hour-long therapy session.

An hour of discussion had passed. Her gait remained stiff as she exited the front door of the hospital, returning to the cold, crisp air outside. Not a speck of sunshine made its way through the dense blanket of cumulus clouds up above, and the once subtle breeze turned into a heavy, powerful wind. Her shoulders stayed glued to her ears and the skin on her crossed arms speckled with goosebumps, even underneath her thick, knitted sweater. She took a shallow breath in, and on her exhale, a cool cloud poured out of her mouth, as if she were exhaling smoke.

Pearl shuffled her feet toward the cramped, crowded parking lot, zig-zagging her way through parked cars. She swung her backpack off to one shoulder and fumbled around for her keys as she approached her old, beat-up truck. She shimmied the key into the lock and pulled the door open. Hopping into the driver's seat, Pearl threw her bag into the passenger's and placed her water bottle into the crumbled bank receipt and gum wrapper-filled cup holder. Before she fastened her seatbelt, she stuck the key into the ignition and turned the tumblers away from her, leaning her chest over the steering wheel while biting her tongue.

*Please start, please start, please start,* she thought to herself, as she listened to the starter click repeatedly. She stepped her foot on and off the pedal. Luckily, after a few seconds of failed battery power, her engine lit up with a mighty roar.

"I knew you had it in you," Pearl said aloud to her truck, patting her hand on the dashboard in praise. She turned on her radio and flipped through the local stations before leaving the structure. Luckily, the rock station was playing one of her favorite punk rock songs, so she did not waste much time looking for something to listen to. She turned the volume up loud, buckled her seatbelt, shifted her truck into reverse, and pulled out of her parking spot, turning the music up even louder as she drove away.

Pearl drove, still, despite the aggressively loud music. Physically still, that is. Her body sat up tall as it rested back on the chair, and her hands remained at ten and two. On the other hand, mentally speaking, stillness had not been heard of in years. Her mind constantly ran wild. She analyzed the last hour of her life. She thought about what she had expressed to Michael during the session, and she thought about what she was able to take away from it. Or rather, a more appropriate question would be what she had not taken away. She debated whether she should continue to drive every week to see Michael or not, considering she had been going for years and had gained close to nothing. No matter how many times she had poured her heart out, she still found herself lost in the dark on a daily basis. She felt stuck, as if the world around her would never change. Her reality slowly grew darker as time passed. *Was it even worth my time or the money I was putting into these sessions?* She wondered, as she had continued commuting there week after week, month after month, and year after year. *When would it end? Would it ever end?* Her mind became adrift. She believed her life was nothing more than excruciating pain and sadness, leaving her empty-hearted and wanting nothing more than to simply end it all. From the moment she woke up in the morning until the moment her head hit her pillow at night and did not sleep for hours on end, she fought in the war against herself with the little force of life she had left.

Within that moment, her mind chattered so loudly that she could no longer hear the music blaring through her pulsing speakers. She stretched her fingers out long and wrapped them over the steering wheel, taking a shallow breath in and out. Gripping her hands firmly, she shifted her gaze over her left shoulder as she sped onto an onramp. Pearl pressed her foot into the pedal as she raced alongside another car in the merging lane next to her. She drove faster, continuously looking back toward her blind spot.

"You have to let me in, bud!" Pearl yelled, annoyed and short-fused. She pressed the pedal closer toward the floor. The car on her left copied.

"Come on! Let me in!" Pearl shouted at the car by her side, as the two lanes quickly became one. It had become clear that the racing car was not slowing down, so Pearl was forced to. She pressed on her breaks and threw a hand in the air.

"Fucking asshole. What is wrong with some people? No one knows how to drive, I swear," she ranted to herself.

Pearl's mood immediately switched as she followed her competition steadily behind. It was not the race itself that pushed her to be upset, nor was it the audacity that some people had that Pearl blamed it on. It had nothing to do with the person on the onramp at all. Really, it was herself that she was angry with, but the lack of mindfulness convinced her otherwise. Her willingness to subconsciously react rather than consciously respond overruled her, and she did not even question it. Instead, she gave her anger permission to run her mind wild.

4

On her drive home from therapy, Pearl stopped by the market, picked up a can of tomato bisque, a block of sharp cheddar cheese, a stick of butter, and a loaf of sourdough bread. Afterward, she drove back home to her one-bedroom apartment. In the woodland outskirts, in a small town called Orchbridge, with a population of about forty thousand people, Pearl lived alone with a single goldfish named Simon. It was not the most ideal living situation, considering she came from the busy, hustling city about an hour away. Yet, her apartment allowed her to save a bit more money on rent.

She walked through her front door, threw her keys on the counter followed by her bag and bottle, set down her groceries, and immediately kicked off her shoes. *Ah shit, I forgot to check the mail,* she thought to herself. Pearl ran back outside to her mailbox, grabbed the few pieces of mail, and made her way back inside. She skimmed through the papers; mostly junk, except for an electricity and an internet bill. Pricier than last month, she noticed, but she had nothing to worry about. Many people around Pearl's age had a difficult time paying bills and supporting themselves. In fact, in this area, although rugged and an hour out of the city, the prices still ran high. It was damn near impossible for someone in their early twenties to live on their own unless they had hit the lottery, worked 24/7, or received an inheritance. In Pearl's case, she had gotten just that.

Pearl Cassel had grown up in a big house in the city with her older brother, Thomas Cassel, and her two hard-working parents, Marissa and David Cassel. Marissa was a hairdresser, while David was an attorney. Pearl was close to her parents and her brother growing up, in fact, one could even say they were the happiest family on the block. However, when Pearl turned eleven, things took a turn for the worst.

One rainy evening, Pearl's parents got a call that their son, Thomas, had overdosed on heroin at a party. He was only seventeen. No one in the family had any idea that he had been using drugs, and his death was completely unexpected. His short life ended tragically, shattering her and her parents' hearts into a million, tiny pieces. It was not long after Thomas' death that Pearl's parents fell into a downward spiral.

After their son's passing, Marissa and David became ticking time bombs of self-destruction. When they got home after a long day of work, they each found themselves constantly sucking their liquor cabinet dry, drowning themselves into oblivion while numbing the horrific loss of their only son. Their actions became so much to deal with, that Pearl found herself distracted from her own sorrow. The once close relationship Pearl had with her parents quickly dwindled into a relationship of pure chaos. For years after, they paid little to no attention to Pearl. Instead, they fed their addiction, toxifying their lives and their reality even more.

Late one night, three days before Pearl's sixteenth birthday, her parents were both killed in a car accident. One car was found t-boned and completely dismantled, and the other car's entire front had been engulfed into its backseat. It took days to identify the victims since both cars had burst into flames. However, once the report released their findings, it was stated that Pearl's parents both had an alcohol level above 2.0. The story is that they ran a red light and drove straight into the middle of a busy intersection, immediately killing an innocent, elderly man driving through. Pearl's father sat in the driver's seat and her mother sat in the passenger's. The report stated that her mother's feet were on the dashboard at the time of the accident, and she had been drinking a beer out of a glass bottle. When their car struck the side of the victim's car, her airbag blew, shooting her knees back into the bottled beer she had in her hand, and shoving the glass bottle down her throat. It shattered instantly inside her. Her dad, on the other hand, slowly suffered his way to the other side, burning alive while stuck in his seat. When Pearl heard the news, she was devastated, distraught, and completely brokenhearted. Unfortunately, though, she was not surprised. That made her almost more sad than the actual death of her parents.

An immense amount of trauma had buried itself deep within Pearl, so much so, that when she tried to think about those times of the past, they were nothing more than a blur. Maybe her brain blocked it out of her memory to keep herself safe and sane. Or maybe, the traumas were so heavy that she subconsciously shoved them down, deeper inside her, so she never had to see them again. Nevertheless, the loss of her family left her feeling hopeless.

After her parents passed, Pearl's aunt, Jen, who also lived in the heart of the city, took custody of Pearl. Pearl spent the last two years of high school slacking off, hanging out with the wrong crowd, and constantly numbing the pain away. After one year of her parent's passing, Pearl found herself so numb from the drugs and alcohol that she consumed every day that any glimpse of reality felt more than overwhelming. She could not bear to deal with the darkness, and shoving it down inside of her felt like the most reliable way to get by. Unfortunately, this method of synthetic healing led her on a downhill spiral, falling deeper into depression with every breath she took. She started to hate the person she was growing into, because her ways to cope were just a constant reminder of the intoxicated past of her parents. She spiraled even further, as her self-judgment and self-hatred grew stronger. Pearl was seventeen when she first tried to commit suicide. Aunt Jen found her overdosing on the bathroom floor with two types of pain medications lying next to her. Immediately after, Aunt Jen checked Pearl into a psych ward. It was not until she attempted suicide the second time a couple years after, that she started to go to see Michael every week.

A few days after Pearl graduated, she moved in with her new boyfriend, Jack. They were only dating for about six months before they started to live together, however, the comfort of someone loving her made Pearl feel more attached than ever. Jack was working as a mechanic during the day, and as a drug dealer by night. He constantly had people coming by their house to buy and test out products, eventually turning their home into a trap house. About two years into her relationship, Pearl's environment grew too toxic for her comfort. She wanted to leave Jack, but she felt manipulated and controlled by him, so much so that she felt totally trapped. Late one night, Pearl tried to make a run for it, until he beat her almost to death. It was not the first time she had been abused by him, but it was the last time before she never had to see him again. Jack was arrested that night, and since then, they haven't seen each other. When Pearl left the hospital a few days after the beating, she moved out of the city and into her new town, Orchbridge.

Despite the disastrous circumstances of Pearl's past, her parents left her with a hefty life insurance check of a half-million dollars. On top of the life insurance, she also held a steady serving job, paying her more than enough to live on without being a listed beneficiary. Hence why she could afford living alone, and of course, acquainted by her pet fish.

She had been in the industry for years, serving throughout high school and after she graduated, eventually working her way up to bartending before she turned twenty-one. In the beginning, she did not mind serving, for it was just another temporary escape from her gut-wrenching reality. She was constantly in the presence of drunk, stupid people that would do anything for another vodka soda double with extra lime. The rude customers were at the top of the totem pole, though. Being cussed out by angry drunks who were 86'd is one thing. Experiencing downright disrespect as if she were not even human, was another. One time, she had a drink thrown at her face; booze, straw, and all. Another time, she had a customer get so mad, that they stood on top of the bar and kicked off condiment caddies and napkin holders, while yelling in rage for being denied another alcoholic beverage. That lasted only a few seconds until the bouncer, EJ, tackled him off the bar top and into the cobblestone floor. That guy was thrown out immediately and hasn't shown his face since. Situations like that did not bother Pearl as much as you would think. After being in the industry so long, one begins to develop a sense of carelessness. However, this other time, a customer called her a peasant girl, and said that she was nothing more than a servant. He said she would never amount to anything except for taking people's orders, and that she was worthless, good for nothing, and pathetic, all while demanding to speak to her manager because of an overcooked burger. She hated to admit it, but that brought her down. She believed him a little, too.

But customers like that were not too common. Overall, the customers were not half bad. The tips were what kept her going. The tips were what kept her in the service industry.

Pearl excelled at what she did. She had a way with people, and despite her depression eating her alive, she always put on a plastic smile, knew exactly what to say, and knew just how to say it. Even when she knew her guests were having a bad day, she did everything in her power to give them an exceptional experience. She listened to their personal complaints, their downfalls and perks of life, and their memorable stories, both good and bad. Some would make her laugh so hard that tears would flow, and others were so sad that she wouldn't dare blink. Other stories made her think, while during others, she would find her mind drifting off into space. Yet, most of the time, the conversations were only had so that the time would pass.

Of course, there were always the creepy, old men that had to throw in their 'two cents' about their opinions of Pearl. She had heard numerous times how beautiful and sexy she was. Awkward, but accepted. She had an overwhelming number of compliments directed at her. Maybe they really thought those things of Pearl, or maybe they simply just wanted to get it in like the horndogs they truly were. Some she appreciated, others she could spit on. There is nothing pleasing of an old man giving her a one-dollar bill shaped as a heart, while shooting the line, "I have a heart-on for you." *Maybe if it were a hundred I would consider,* she would joke to herself.

It was not until the last two years that serving had become an energy-sucking vampire. She listened to the sob stories of everyone around her, all while pretending to care. Over time, the voices of these emotional people explaining their struggles to Pearl became a constant aggravation. Nobody ever asked her how she was doing, and she felt under-appreciated despite all the hard work and commitment she had constantly put into her current and previous jobs. She felt unbalanced, as if she were giving too much of herself, both physically and mentally. Ultimately, while her personal struggles grew darker and the battle to fight became harder, she began to grow careless of her customer service and if it was good or not. She was not herself there, or anywhere for that matter. She constantly felt tired and had no energy to give to anyone. Pearl felt simply drained, but she had no idea as to where she would go from here. She believed to be stuck, once again, yet she still managed to uphold the responsibility of living in a life that she so desperately wanted to end.

Pearl's story unfolding the way it has, has ultimately led her down a path of depression and despair. For years, she remained stuck, lost, and trapped in the outskirts of her own mind. Despite the unphased persona she portrayed to the world, she had yet to find happiness. She believed herself to be a victim. Everyone and everything were out to get her, and no matter what she did, the darkness continued to creep over her even more. The only way to solve her problems was to simply forget about them, she believed. To bury them deep inside her, and to never dig them back up again. She believed that her problems would never find her if she continued to run away from them, suppress them, or take something to forget them. However, a band-aid can only mask the pain for so long.

5

Pearl crumpled the junk mail and tossed it into the trash, while setting aside her two bills. She put her groceries away, grabbed a pickle out of the fridge, and flopped down onto her couch. In front of her was a narrow coffee table covered with crumbs, books, papers for writing, papers for rolling, and more. Off to the side, rested her journal. It was a hardback, thick with lined papers and pen marks scratched all over it. One thing she did gain from her therapy sessions with Michael was the act of journaling. Michael encouraged her to get into the habit of journaling every so often, so she did.

She reached over and grabbed her journal and pen, opened it up, and started flipping through the pages. Pearl never felt encouraged to go back and read what she wrote in her journal. But for whatever reason, her curiosity got the best of her that day. Pearl found herself reading her written thoughts and feelings from the past few years. She flipped randomly to a few entries and found herself locked into what she read.

<u>Wednesday, 1/3/18, 7:50pm</u>

Can't help but feel my ending is near. I have little to no hope left for myself. Smiling cannot seem to hide my true emotions that are eating me alive. I cannot help but feel my depression take over my entire existence. Every day that comes and goes is harder than the one before.

Friday, 6/8/18, 6:26pm

I am so fucking over with what this life has become. The amount of sadness and frustration I feel within is unbearable, and I don't know how much longer I can last. There is nothing for me to live for. All I want is to be happy. Why can't I?

Wednesday, 11/13/19, 11:21pm

Why do I even bother writing in this thing? Nothing has changed except for the fact that I am only growing sadder and more hopeless. I don't know what I did to deserve the hand that I have been dealt. Just kill me already. I would not mind.

Pearl exhaled a long, heavy sigh. She tapped the top of the pen against the journal as she continued flipping through the pages. Finally, she reached an empty page. She stared blankly at the page while the page stared blankly back. Yet, before she put pen to paper, she thought of something that could help procrastinate. She rested the pen on the page and closed the journal.

Pearl picked up her phone and called one of her friends, Ella, who she had known from senior year of high school. Ella was one of the only people Pearl knew from school that had moved to Orchbridge, too. They weren't very close, in fact they weren't even really alike. However, the company of someone from the past felt comforting, and despite their shallow relationship, it made Pearl's time go by even faster. Ella was a superficial, self-centered young woman. She was one of those people who was always getting into trouble and was constantly down for the get down. Yet, one thing they did have in common was the desire to escape reality by intoxicating their minds. Together, they were always under the influence, drowning their problems with poison. Ella, too, had her own shadows buried deep within. Yet, unlike Pearl, who was at least aware of her sadness, Ella was far from seeing hers, in fact it would take another lifetime for Ella to remember her truth. Until then, in this life, she was just trying to get by the best she could, using the most synthetic ingredients possible.

"Hello?" Ella answered the phone after three rings.

"Hey girl, what are you up to tonight?" Pearl bit her nails.

"Trying to figure that out right now, actually. What about you?"

"I was thinking about going to Spark's tonight. Would you be down?"

"Yeah, I'm down with that! I'll pick you up?" Ella offered.

"Sounds good. See you around…?"

"8:30 or 9:00?"

"Perfect," Pearl responded, relieved for the soon escape.

"Ugh, thank God you called. Today has been a fucking day. I'm ready to let loose tonight."

"I feel that," Pearl snickered, "I could definitely use a couple of drinks."

"Me too. Okay cool, I'll see you soon."

The two of them hung up the phone. Pearl looked over at the ticking clock below her television and saw that she had about three to four hours to kill until then. She glanced back down at her waiting-to-be-written-in journal and moaned loudly, as if she was being forced to write something down. So, she did, only so her conscience would stop pestering her about it.

Friday, 2/7/20, 5:13pm

Went to see Michael again today and I feel like at this point, we are just catching up with my life rather than fixing the problems I have. The hole in my heart is too big to ever be healed, too deep to ever fill up, and too dark to ever see the light again. Nobody understands me. I'm tired of living this life.

Pearl wrote in her journal for the hundred-something time, filling it more with negativity and worry, so much so that it grew heavier over time with every entry she wrote. As if the world owed her something, she convinced herself that her sorrows stood at the center of the universe. But even she was not that special, nobody in this life was. It was only a matter of time before she figured that out.

6

A couple of drinks turned into three, four, or five. Maybe even six or seven? They sat in the center of Spark's Bar and Lounge for hours on end. It was the first time Pearl and Ella had seen each other in a few months, so they discussed random banter to cease the silence. Pearl didn't really care about having a good conversation, sucking down her sorrows with tequila was her number one priority.

Spark's was nothing special. It was your basic small-town dive bar. There were old, signed dollar bills and tacky, flashing signs hanging along the dark walls. The barstools squeaked every time someone moved to reposition their ass, and the bar top had glass rings stained into the tarnished wood. Spark's even had games like billiards and shuffleboards in the darkest corner of the joint, and there were about ten tall, round tables, each with two chairs, that sat throughout the pub. On a weekend, this place was the place to be, especially if one was looking to wipe their memory clean. The weekdays were quieter, but once in a blue moon, the creatures of the night came out to play. It was always entertaining, but sometimes, it could be downright scary.

First, they started with tequila shots. Pearl had salt and lime, while Ella had it straight, because she was way too advanced for training wheels. Then, Ella had another tequila shot and a house margarita on the side for a chaser, while Pearl ordered a single margarita, garnished with salt and lime. After that, Pearl ordered another margarita while Ella switched to a vodka soda. Later, Pearl ordered a plate of nachos and a cerveza, while Ella went for two more drinks on her own. The two of them went from the girls who kept to themselves, to *those* girls at the bar. At least Ella did, anyway.

7

Pearl generally came off as reserved, being the introvert she was. On the outside, she appeared strong in her skin, perfectly masking her traumas like she had never once felt pain in her life. Yet, on the inside, lived a sad soul who appeared to be lost, heartbroken, deeply depressed, and inconsolable. She did a good job at keeping that part of herself hidden for only herself and sometimes Michael to see. But of course, alcohol always had a way of making those things a little more visible.

She handled her alcohol well, for the most part. She kept her head on her shoulders and respected her limits. When she intoxicated her mind, she was still quiet and tame. The only noticeable difference, besides the occasional slurring, the heavy eyes, and distorted vision, was that she became much more vulnerable and emotional than her sober mind would be. She drank just enough to enjoy herself and forget about her struggles, but still have awareness of her surroundings. At least as aware as one could be despite being so disconnected to their higher self. This was unlike her friend Ella, who became the egocentric, know-it-all, loud, heartless broad at the bar.

"Another round, bartender!" Ella shouted, waving her hand in the air to grab his attention.

"No, we are fine right now," Pearl said, as she reached for Ella's hand and pulled it back down by her side. "Maybe a glass of water would be better."

The bartender came over with an eyebrow raised as he looked into Ella's glazed eyes, setting down two glasses of cold water.

"Thank you," Pearl said politely.

"Where are our drinks?" Ella slurred obnoxiously.

"These are our drinks," Pearl stated, taking a sip of her glass.

"This is water." Ella stared, dumbfounded.

"Yes, you are correct," Pearl replied sarcastically.

"You're no fun." Ella rolled her eyes as she took a sip of water. She rested her elbows on the bar top and slouched over, her head resting in her hands. She swung her feet back and forth and swayed her hips, twisted her stool, and pouted like a child. Pearl took another sip, too. They sat quietly for a moment.

Pearl's eyes wandered over her shoulder as she turned the stool. In the corner playing pool, she noticed two tall, wide, middle-aged men. One wore a trucker's hat and the other let his thinning hair out freely, and they both had a single, enormous 'ab' hanging over their belt buckles. Pearl thought of plumbers when she saw them, because when they bent over to shoot, their ass cracks would wave hello. The men kept to themselves, minding their own business with a couple of brews in hand. In the other corner, an older man sat alone with a pint of beer, watching the news on the janky flat screen hanging on the wall in front of him. Sitting at the end of the bar, about five stools down from Pearl, was a man and woman, mid-thirties, who were loudly making small talk with glasses of wine beneath their noses. Pearl wondered about them. *Had just started dating? Maybe it was their first date?* From their conversations, it sounded like it could be. They both had asked each other what they did for a living, and they both discussed their personal milestones in life. They spoke so loudly that Pearl could not help but eavesdrop. Beside Ella, about three stools down, sat a single young man, maybe barely thirty, who was also watching the news on another hanging flat screen. About two seats after that, at the very end of the bar, sat another man by himself, middle-aged and thin like a string bean. He slouched his shoulders over and kept his gaze down on his phone, while snacking on chicken strips and sipping on his whiskey. For a Friday night at Spark's, it was oddly slow.

Pearl swung her body back around to face the bar, taking another sip of water. She glanced over at Ella who was sitting with her eyes buried in her phone.

"What time is it?" Pearl asked Ella.

"Ten fiiity-seven."

"Really?" Pearl's eyes opened wide and then fell heavy once again. "It's not even eleven yet? This night is dragging."

"I know, right?" Ella snorted, taking another sip of water, and swaying back and forth in her seat. This forced Pearl to sit on the edge of her seat, for Ella's swaying made her nervous. She would not be surprised if she would fall off the stool; it would not be the first time.

"It is totally dragging. This place is always busy, but there is nobody here tonight. No one to talk to," Ella continued.

Pearl crinkled her eyebrows, smirked, and shot Ella a glance. Ella looked back, realizing what she had said.

"Except for you, obviously," Ella said. "I meant that there are no guys around here." She slammed her water glass down so loud that it caught the attention of a couple of people sitting at the bar next to them.

"Well what were you expecting to happen?"

"I don't know. But what I do know is that I haven't had sex in forever."

Pearl laughed awkwardly. Dating wasn't even a thought that crossed Pearl's mind. She was single and relishing in it, and considering she had gotten out of an abusive relationship herself only a couple years back, she had no desire to put herself out there. It was her first long-term relationship she had ever had, shattering her heart even more than it already was. Just another reason to obliviate her mind.

"Oh, Pearl, I meant to ask you, Avery, Celeste, and I are going up to the city for a night to go see Shackled Shadow. Avery's sister was supposed to uh, supposed to..." she paused for a moment, as the alcohol took her mind adrift.

Pearl raised an eyebrow. "Supposed to...?"

Ella recollected her thoughts. "Supposed to come, but she can't

43

anymore. She got scheduled to work last minute. So, we have an extra ticket. You in?"

*Shackled Shadow? Fuck, it did sound tempting.* Shackled Shadow was one of Pearl's all-time favorite punk rock bands. They expressed her emotions in ways she would never be able to. She enjoyed listening to music that sounded like it was listening to her. "Salivating Darkness" was her go-to song when she was feeling down. So, one would say she listened to it often.

"What day?" Pearl asked.

"The concert is next Friday night. We are leaving in the morning and making a day of it. Come with us!"

Pearl was seriously considering it. That was until she remembered she was scheduled to see Michael that Friday, late afternoon. *But how many chances would I have to go see Shackled Shadow again?* She wondered. But then she remembered that she pretty much had no other choice but to see Michael. Pearl had a history of not showing up for her appointments. She would completely ghost Michael out of sheer dejection and hopelessness, so much so that the last time she did, police showed up at her front door and took her in for suicide watch. And that was not the first time, either. She could not afford to miss another therapy session. Being admitted back to the hospital for a few days sounded as appetizing as taking a bite out of an onion.

"I can't go," Pearl groaned. She was truly upset that she could not.

"Why not?"

"I... I have plans that day," Pearl stuttered.

"What kind of plans?" Ella asked interrogatively.

Pearl kept her personal business to herself, yet the sudden interest Ella had when she said she couldn't go made Pearl feel wanted. The mystery of Pearl's plans and the alcohol that bubbled within her was just enough to unleash the truth.

"I have to go see my therapist that day. It's, uh, kind of mandatory."

Ella looked puzzled. "Therapy? You go to therapy?"

"Yeah, ha, ha, " Pearl laughed, unsure of what to say next. She had no idea what Ella's response would be, and the unknown frightened her. Yet, Ella seemed interested.

"I didn't know you went to therapy. Therapy for what?"

Pearl grew quiet. It was not every day that someone asked her why she was going to therapy, or rather, why she was crazy, according to her deceiving mind. She did not know what she should say, but she felt like this was her chance to say something. Or maybe that was the alcohol talking.

"Ha…" Pearl paused with hesitance. "I've been going for a while now. I'm uh, kind of fucked up." She laughed aloud again. She always did when she felt uncomfortable.

"What is going on, Pearl?" Ella asked with concern, like she was genuinely curious. She placed her hands over Pearl's and looked at her with full attention.

"I just…" Pearl hesitated, her breath flowing short through her quivering lips. "I just have a lot of traumas. I've been going for years. I've just been in a dark place ever since my brother and parents passed away. I feel like I've gone through so much so young, that I don't know how to handle it. And with Jack, too. I just can't seem to let go of the past. Sometimes I wonder why I'm still even here."

"Why do you say that?"

"I mean—" Pearl choked while her eyes engulfed with tears. She could not hold them back, so she stopped trying. She felt overwhelmingly vulnerable. "I feel uncomfortable living the life I do. I feel like I can never catch a break. I swear the world painted a giant, red target on my back. It has just been one thing after another after another, to the point where it's like, why go on, you know? I just—I just can't be happy."

Ella closed her eyes and patted Pearl's hands, smiling softly. "I know how you feel, Pearl. I've been there."

"Oh yeah?" Pearl asked hopefully.

"Totally. I had this cat one time. His name was Ronny. I had him pretty much my whole life as a kid. About twelve or thirteen years. He died freshmen year of high school and I legit thought I was going to kill myself. I was so sad. Grief is a hard thing to deal with," Ella slurred, while stealing a nacho from Pearl's basket.

Pearl stared at her blankly with her jaw dropped, while tears continued rolling down her face.

"I mean," Ella started, then paused as she threw the chip in her big mouth. She crunched the nacho loudly, as she continued to speak once again. She meant to say, "it's just part of life, you know?" But instead, she said "iz juss parta life, ya' know?"

As inconsiderate and shallow as Ella was, she did have a point. Death is, as a matter of fact, a part of life. That was probably one of the most intelligent things she had said all evening. However, Pearl was immediately defensive with Ella for comparing her loss of her cat, Ronny, to the loss of her brother, parents, and the rest of her traumas. *As if her pain even came close to mine,* Pearl thought.

"Yeah, I know it is a part of life. But that doesn't mean I'm not allowed to feel the way I do."

"Oh, come on Pearl, it can't be that bad," Ella said, minimizing Pearl's feelings as if she had no reason for them.

Pearl's tears came to a halt as she looked at Ella, shocked, and displeased with her response. She wanted to ask her, "did you seriously just say that to me?" But instead, she remained quiet.

"I know your brother and parents died, and I'm so sorry for that. And I know you went through some shit with Jack. But those both happened years ago, Pearl. You just have to get over it," Ella continued, her eyes almost rolling in the back of her head. "Do what I do, drink your problems away. The best way to solve your problems is to simply not deal with them. Bury that shit. You know what we need? Another tequila shot. Bartender!" Ella yelled for the man behind the bar.

"Are—are you serious?"

"Yeah, it's time for another drink." The bartender set down two more tequilas. Ella picked up her glass and prepared to cheers, while Pearl sat still, mind boggled as to why she just poured her heart out to someone who clearly did not give a shit. She felt completely humiliated and embarrassed that she ever said anything, and she immediately wished she could take it back. *What is wrong with me? What is wrong with her?* She thought to herself.

"Pearl?"

"What?"

"Cheers?"

"Oh, sorry." Pearl picked up the shot and pushed it into Ella's. They both tapped them back onto the bar top, and then tossed them back into their gullets. Pearl tossed the lime in her mouth immediately while Ella licked her lips clean.

"So," Ella turned back toward Pearl, "can't you just skip therapy that day?"

Pearl, who was internally steaming with rage, upheld her polite persona. "I wish I could, but it's kind of mandatory I go. It's hard to explain."

"Sounds pretty lame if you ask me." Ella rolled her eyes, turned her head away from Pearl, and strummed her fingers on top of the bar. Suddenly, her phone lit up with an incoming call. "I have to take this," she stated, jumping out of her seat. Ella checked out of her and Pearl's conversation, pulled her long, blonde hair off to one side, and put her phone to her ear, as she stumbled away from the bar, leaving Pearl in the dust. Pearl sat alone with disgust, then turned back toward the bartender.

"I'll cash out, please."

"Are you guys paying together or separate?"

"Separate."

8

Pearl got a taxi home that evening and tossed and turned in bed all night. The next morning, she awoke with a horrible hangover.

She lied limp in her bed, her back sunken deep into her mattress. Her eyes began to peel open slowly, one eye more open than the other, as she rubbed her crusted lashes with the palms of her hands. Her ceiling fan was turned off, yet she could not help but notice how fast it spun above her. The whole room did somersaults and her head pounded harder than a sledgehammer.

Her awareness slowly returned to center. She reminisced on her night before with Ella, the amount of alcohol they had consumed, how abnormally slow the place was, and how unsettling creepy the cab driver home appeared to be. As those thoughts passed, her mind immediately remembered the conversation she and Ella had at the bar. She remembered how she completely opened her heart to Ella and revealed parts of herself that she never thought she would. She exposed certain shadows within her darkness that burned when subjected to light. For once, she stepped into a space of vulnerability, yet the ears she spoke to, voluntarily muted her cries. Her words were unappreciated, unheard, and undervalued, and she found herself shocked to feel even lower than she had already been. It felt more than unnerving.

Pearl slowly rolled over onto her left side. She shifted her gaze toward her side table and tapped her phone's screen. It read 6:33am.

"Ugh," Pearl groaned. She pulled the sheets back over her head, curled up into a ball, and fell back to sleep.

A couple more hours passed as Pearl's eyelids began to open gradually once again. This time, her awakening was more abrupt than before. The intoxicating feeling from that night felt more than enough to wake her up, and this time, keep her up. She laid flaccid, as if she was on her deathbed. At least it felt like it, anyway. Her hangover began to make itself more prominent as her stomach churned. At that moment, the sensation of nausea took the stage, capturing her attention more than anything else in her world. Without even checking the time, Pearl shot up and out of her bed and sprinted to the toilet.

This would not be the first time Pearl found herself face first into a toilet bowl from a night of intoxication. Pearl dropped to her knees, lifted the toilet seat, and immediately projectile vomited stomach acid. Bile slithered up her throat and out of her mouth. With every moment of pause to recollect her breath, she was engulfed with the fumes of sitting toilet water. With her second inhale, her stomach clenched yet again, throwing up practically nothing. After a few more purges of bile and whatever other liquid was occupying itself in her belly, she gasped for a deep breath in, receiving nothing but a trapped airway. She choked, gasping again, gripping the toilet seat with her fingers and thumbs, yet still no inhale breath. Her whole body convulsed once more until another rush of bile raced up and out of her body. Finally, she was gifted with a full breath in, and a relieving breath out.

Pearl had dry heaved so much in those short seconds, but it was nothing she was not already used to. She sat there defeated, her chin resting on her arms that draped over the toilet seat. Her mouth lay slightly open as she inhaled and exhaled deeply, while her bitter saliva hung from her bottom lip, dripping into the water below.

She realized that there was nothing left inside of her. No matter how hard she tried, she had nothing more to give, both physically and mentally. She sat back up and off the toilet, pressing her back against the wall behind her. She sat there, hunched over, wide-eyed and traumatized as she stared at the toilet bowl with despair. She brought her knees into her chest and wrapped her arms around herself, giving herself a great, big hug. She tucked her chin into her chest and hid her face, while she sobbed like a baby, completely fearful of and terrorized by the life she lived.

9

As the day went on, Pearl found herself nestled on her couch, introverting herself from the outside world. She lay bundled under one of her favorite fluffy blankets, with a pair of fluffy socks squeezing her feet.

Pearl flipped through her television guide in hopes to distract her monkey mind with even more mass programming. However, her desperate need for distraction had her subconsciously focusing on her problems more than ever. While she pressed the buttons on her remote, she found herself in a trance of despair, not even reading the channels on the screen. She recapped her evening with Ella, once again, not believing the audacity that Ella had. Pearl's thoughts became harsher, as she continued to judge herself like a movie critic. She thought to herself, *why did I tell Ella any of that stuff? Why did I open myself up to someone who could care less if I am even here or not? What does she think of me, now? Why do I have to be such a fucking idiot, sometimes?*

Pearl spent her entire day off pitying herself. She was utterly convinced that the world was out to get her, and that nobody on the planet could ever relate to her or the pain she felt on a daily basis. She was a true victim of her own harsh reality.

10

A week and a half passed by. Nothing too exciting those past eleven days; just the same as they usually were. She had worked thirty to forty hours, and she spent another hour with Michael, which meant no Shackled Shadow. Pearl did not care too much, though, in fact hanging out with Ella after the night at Spark's was the last thing she wanted to do. In Pearl's free time, she stayed in the comfort of her own apartment, letting the days pass her by, miserable in her own skin.

It was a Wednesday morning, Pearl woke up at nine, and then rolled out of bed at eleven. She left her bed unmade, kept her shades closed, and left her unfolded laundry on her chair for the sixth day in a row. However, she did get some of her chores done.

She washed her pile of dishes that had been sitting for five days, she mopped her kitchen floor, and she fed Simon a little bit extra than usual. After her chores, she made herself some breakfast; one egg cooked over medium and a glass of orange juice on the side. About thirty minutes passed, and she left her egg half eaten and her juice untouched.

*Knock, knock, knock.* Pearl's front door called for her. She peeled her body off her couch and dragged her feet to answer. She peeked through the peephole, and noticed it was her Aunt. Pearl unlocked the door and welcomed her in.

"Hey Aunt Jen, what's up? Is everything okay?"

"Hey!" Aunt Jen slid past Pearl and made her way inside with her hands full of groceries. Aunt Jen had long, brown hair that hovered just over her hips, dark, brown eyes underneath her oversized, square-framed glasses, and perfectly straight teeth. She appeared fit, health conscious, and more than energized. "Did you forget that I was stopping by?"

"Uh—of course not," Pearl lied. She had one hundred percent forgotten. Pearl followed Aunt Jen to the kitchen and watched her unload the brown paper bags.

"The farmer's market had so many deals today. I grabbed you some lettuce, some apples, some oranges, some bananas..." Aunt Jen pulled them out of the bag. "I also got you this!" Excited, she pulled out a bag of roasted, salted almonds from a local supplier; Pearl's favorite.

"Ah, wow, thank you so much," Pearl said with little to no life in her voice. "You did not have to do that."

Aunt Jen stopped unloading and looked over at Pearl. She lifted her hands and touched the sides of Pearl's face.

"Hm," she murmured. "How are you doing? Did you see Michael last week?"

"Yes," Pearl replied, turning her head away.

Aunt Jen grabbed Pearl's chin and brought it back to center. "And how was it?"

"The same as it usually is." Pearl pulled her head away again, taking a step back. "I don't even know why I'm still seeing him."

"Because he is helping you, Pearl."

"Is that why I am still seeing him? Wouldn't you think if therapy were actually helping me that I wouldn't still be going after all this time?"

Aunt Jen fell quiet for a few moments. Then, she stated, "It's only temporary, Pearl. I promise."

Pearl chuckled out loud, as if Aunt Jen cracked a joke. Pearl had no desire to continue talking about herself, so she changed the subject before Aunt Jen had anything more to say. "How much do I owe you for all this?"

Aunt Jen snickered. "Don't even try."

"Thank you." Pearl smiled, and even though she felt unhappy, she was ever so grateful to have someone in her life that genuinely gave a fuck about her.

After unloading the groceries, Pearl and Aunt Jen made their way over to the couch.

"So, what are your plans for the rest of the day?" Aunt Jen asked.

"Just lounging until work tonight."

"How's work been lately?"

Pearl thought about her question, for a moment. "Work's been good," she lied, "but—"

"Wait, wait, wait, where's your remote?" Aunt Jen interrupted. "Did you hear that?"

Pearl shook her head side to side as she handed the remote to her aunt. Aunt Jen turned up the volume and focused on the television in front of them. On the TV showed a news anchor reporting yet another missing person in the area.

"Have you heard about this?" Aunt Jen asked Pearl.

"No, what is it? I haven't been watching the news lately."

"Another person reported missing. There have been so many lately around here. They have been finding bodies around the city, with no evidence of who or what did it to them. They even found a body in Orchbridge a week ago. It's so fucking weird. Do you still carry pepper spray in your bag?"

"Yes."

"Good. You don't know who's out there. Don't trust anybody, even if they seem like the nicest person you have ever met."

Pearl rolled her eyes. *Did you forget how old I am?* "I know, Aunt Jen. But if I am being truthful, nothing really scares me anymore." Pearl believed it to be true, but she could only convince herself for so long.

# THE FOREST

1

A couple of weeks later, Pearl found herself in the city picking up Aunt Jen from the airport, who had just returned from a three-day business trip. Jen unbuckled her seatbelt as they pulled up to her house.

"I'm happy there was no traffic at least," Pearl mentioned, parking in the driveway and turning off the engine.

"Me too. Thank you so much for the ride, Pearl. You want to come in for a bit?"

"Of course, I wasn't doing anything anyway. And no, not today, I think I'm going to just head home." Pearl's anxiety and depression felt more prominent than ever that day. She thought doing this favor would distract her temporarily from her monkey mind, but instead, the drive alone into the city sent her spiraling. She wanted nothing more than to be home, alone, and in her own bed.

"You sure? Are you okay?" Aunt Jen asked Pearl with worry in her eyes.

"Ugh," Pearl rolled her eyes. "I'm fine." Pearl hated being asked if she was okay. She hated talking about herself, and the spotlight simply terrified her. She brushed off the question, set her elbow down on the center console, and rested her chin on her knuckles, keeping her eyes away from Aunt Jen.

"Pearl."

Pearl took a deep breath in through her nose, and a deeper breath out of her nose. She turned her head toward her aunt and flashed a slight smile. "I'm fine, Aunt Jen. Really. It's just one of those days."

Aunt Jen smiled back, gave her a kiss on the cheek, and stepped out of the truck. "I love you. Thanks again for the ride, text me when you get home. And drive safe!"

"Love you too," Pearl responded, nodding her head toward Aunt Jen. Pearl went to start the truck once again, spinning the key two or three times away from her face. After a few gut-wrenching clicks, the engine roared. Relieved, Pearl shifted into reverse, backed out of the driveway, and drove away.

2

Pearl drove along the long highway without another car in sight. The highway traveled through the depths of a forest, covering the sides of the road with nothing but trees. She found her mind adrift, gazing up at the blanket of grey clouds covering the sky as she sped eighty miles-per-hour. Suddenly, with the blink of an eye, the road went from empty to bumper to bumper traffic. *What's going on?* Pearl thought. She stretched her neck out her window to try to see around the semi-truck in front of her. As the road slowly turned around the bend, Pearl noticed orange cones directing everyone off the road ahead, leading her into unknown territory. This detour took her about a mile off away from the highway, deeper into the forest. Unclear as to where this road would take her, she continued to follow the cars ahead, like the blind leading the blind.

For about fifteen minutes, the cars crept forward, one after another. The fifteen minute detour felt like hours to Pearl. As she followed the cones, she found herself lost between the voices of her chattering thoughts. Today felt harder than others, and her anxiety was at an all-time high. She could barely breathe underneath her seatbelt, and her stomach felt like it was crawling up her throat. She tried taking a breath, although shallow, to calm her nerves. Instead, a tear trickled down her cheek and off her chin, leaving her with her chilling thoughts that flooded in one ear and out the other. *I can't do this anymore,* she thought to herself. *I don't want to live anymore. I can't live anymore.*

As the cars drove deeper through the trees, a giant, orange sign became clear at an upcoming fork in the road. As Pearl drove closer, she noticed the detour sign directing traffic to the left, back toward another alternative highway onramp. As the cars crept forward, stopping one by one at the stop sign before they turned back to the highway, Pearl's heart began to pound out of her chest. Lost in her thoughts, at the very last second possible, Pearl jolted out of her left turn, turned to the right, and drove deeper into the forest with only one intention in mind.

She drove into the unknown and away from civilization for about eight more miles, passing nothing but tree, after tree. Some were tall, some were short, some had more leaves on their branches, and others did not. Some had trunks as big as an average sized car, and some were so thin, Pearl could wrap her arms all the away around. Nevertheless, the trees created a massive, green blanket overhead. For miles, there was nothing but trees as far as the eye could see. And despite the differences each tree portrayed, they each casted a unique, mysterious complexion.

Suddenly, the road's surface faded from pavement to dirt and rock. Pearl found herself bouncing up and down in her seat along the skinny dirt road. As she journeyed deeper into the forest, she eventually pulled off, down a smaller road that looked as if it had not been used in years. This road to nowhere felt unsettling, yet it called to her like a howling wolf in the night. She did not come as far as she had to turn back now. She set her mind to end it all, in that moment, and not a moment less. She yearned to flee from the darkness that had taken over her whole life; a darkness that spread like the plague, constantly polluting her mind with sick, negative thoughts, so much so that her mind had become so contaminated, she grew hollow. Depression had grown over both her mind and body like layers of an onion, constantly stacking layers on top of layers, ultimately covering the light that shined within her. The thought of suicide felt more appetizing than taking another breath on earth. Pearl inched her way through the tunnel of trees, her truck rocking back and forth, until suddenly, the road came to an end.

3

Pearl parked her truck and turned off the engine. She reached for her bag sitting in the passenger's seat, grabbed her smartphone, and tapped the screen. Only 3% battery life remaining. Pearl rolled her eyes, tossed her phone back into her bag, hopped out of the truck, and slammed the door closed behind her.

Trees with tops higher than she could see stretched up tall at the end of the dirt road. Pearl looked up at the trees, watching the leaves rustle against one another as they danced with the subtle wind. The air felt so chill and crisp that goosebumps speckled her body. She grabbed onto opposite elbows, let out a mighty exhalation, and wandered into the trees, leaving her truck behind.

Pearl prowled through the tall tree trunks, crunching fallen leaves underneath her feet with every step she took. Eventually, she reached the edge of a cliff. From afar, the view gifted her with a beautiful mountain range, covered by a sea of green trees. The hillside was illuminated by a golden stream of light, breaking through the patches of clouds above. Below, the cliff dropped straight down at least two hundred feet. At the bottom rested more trees and large, grey boulders in between. Pearl kept her gaze down, involuntarily holding her breath as she contemplated her life and if it was worth living anymore. No one was here to stop her. All she had to do was jump, and then it would be over. Her pain, her suffering, her constant darkness choking the life out of her, would all come to an end. *I would be free,* she thought to herself. *Free from this life, forever. I just have to do it.*

Pearl stepped closer toward the edge, peeking her head over toward the bottom even more. Suddenly, a small rock rolled under her foot and off the edge, falling into the pit. She stepped back, grounding her feet firmly down into the cliffside, gazing back up and out at the view. She took a deep breath in, and a deeper breath out, releasing a tear from each eye. *I can do this,* she thought to herself once again. She closed her eyes tight, blinked them back open, and before she could make her next move, her eyes caught sight of a giant butterfly fluttering in the distance. She squinted her eyes to get a better look, until suddenly, the butterfly fluttered its way through the sea of trees, against the chilled breeze, until it landed softly on a rock at the base of Pearl's feet.

"What the...?" Pearl whispered out loud. "What are you doing here little guy?" The butterfly remained in its place, flapping its wings ever so lightly. Pearl dropped to her knees and stuck out her index finger. She brought her finger to the butterfly, and without hesitation, the butterfly crawled up onto it. Pearl's eyes opened wide with disbelief. She stood back up onto her feet and brought the butterfly close, examining its beauty from every direction. It was blue, and it had a black outline, with white and gold speckles. It was unlike anything Pearl had ever seen before, and to hold something so beautiful in such a dark time provided her with a breath of fresh air. In the stillness and the magic, the anxiety bundled in her stomach faded away, and the tightness in her chest released. Her monkey mind grew quiet for a moment, and the only thing engulfing her was the moment of presence. Instantly, the butterfly fluttered up and off her finger, making its way back into the endless sea of trees. Pearl followed it with teary, yet hopeful eyes. *How could something so remarkably beautiful strike at such a dark time? Was it a sign from the Universe? A sign from God? Or was it simply a coincidence?* Whatever it was, whether it meant something or not, Pearl stepped back from the cliff's edge, dropped down to her knees, and buried her face into her hands, releasing one of the biggest cries she had in years.

4

Pearl wiped the tears from her frosted face and sniffled her congested, red nose. She lifted her face out of her hands and stared off into the distance once again, her eyes glistening over in a daze. *This is not my time,* she thought to herself, deciding against her plans of suicide. *I cannot give up. Not this time.*

Pearl pushed herself back onto her feet and sauntered her way back through the forest. Finally, her truck became clear in sight. She pulled open the door, jumped into the driver's seat, and slammed the door behind her. She slid her key into the tumblers, yet all she received back was the ticking of the old, worn-out, used, and abused battery.

"Ugh, oh no. Please turn on," she begged aloud. "Please, please, please."

*Click, click, click, click,* the battery ticked.

Pearl brought the key back to center, giving her truck and herself a moment to breathe. After a few moments of silence, she tried again, turning the tumblers.

*Click, click, click, click, click.* Pearl stepped on and off the petal, giving some gas in hopes of a spark.

"Come on, don't do this to me right now!" Pearl yelled at her truck, gripping the steering wheel tight between her freezing fingers.

*Click, click, click,* it responded. Pearl untwisted the key and sat back in her chair.

"Fuck," she whispered to herself, as she closed her eyes and pressed the back of her skull into the headrest. She blinked her eyes open once again, snatched her backpack out of the passenger seat, and dropped it down on her lap. She fumbled through her bag in search of her phone. When she felt it, she pulled it out and tapped the screen. With no response, she tapped it again, and again.

"Are you serious, right now?" She asked her phone as if it had an answer. Alas, she found herself staring at her own eyes through the black mirror. Just like her car battery, her phone had died, too. She knocked the back of her head into the headrest, lifting her chin up high toward the sky in hopes of a break from the world. "This can't be happening right now."

Pearl could feel her blood boiling hot, cooking her insides to a crisp. She had two options, one of which she decided against only moments earlier. So, Pearl kicked her door open once again, grabbed her backpack and water bottle, slammed the door closed, and securely locked it behind her. She shoved her bottle into her small, yet roomy bag, swung both straps over both of her shoulders, and dragged her feet back through the forest toward the main road. She needed to get into town, and the only way to do so was to walk. So, she abandoned her car and did just that.

The breeze grew colder as Pearl made her way onto the paved road, eventually finding herself ambling alongside the long, quiet road. One way headed north, and the other way headed south, this road drove through the middle of nowhere. It stretched miles and miles away from the nearest town and into the mysterious unknown.

She wandered.

5

Pearl had been walking alone for about an hour through the cold forest. She stuck her thumb out for a few cars that drove by, yet none stopped to offer her a ride. She pulled on her bag's straps and hugged her shoulders close to her ears. As the day slowly morphed into the evening, the temperature grew even colder. *Why didn't I just do it? I wouldn't be walking in the middle of nowhere if I had,* she thought. Suddenly, around the corner behind her, she heard another car approaching for the first time in over ten minutes. Pearl spun around and stuck her thumb out into the road, hoping that whoever it was could give her the help she had been waiting for. Alas, the car drove faster, passing her by.

"Fuck," she spoke under her breath, frozen in place. Her eyes followed the speeding car, until suddenly, the sound of another engine roared behind her. From behind sped a nice, clean, luxury vehicle through the lonesome forest. Yet, as the car drove closer, it began to slow down, until it came to a complete stop next to Pearl. The tinted window rolled down, and a deep voice yelled out.

"You need a ride?" A man shouted to Pearl. He appeared middle-aged, maybe forties or fifties. He had a five o'clock shadow, slicked-back hair over his skull, wore a nice, fitted black suit, and he had a look in his eyes that was beautifully unique.

She lowered her thumb and walked up to the passenger door. "Yes, sir, I do."

"Where ya' headed?" The mysterious man asked.

"Just into town, here. My truck broke down about a mile or two up the road."

"You didn't think about calling a car service?"

"My phone died, too."

"Of course, it did," the man responded, chuckling to himself. "Well, you're in luck, little lady. I am headed into town, too. Make yourself comfortable."

"Thank you." Pearl murmured.

The stranger unlocked the door from the driver's door, inviting Pearl inside. Pearl opened the door and hopped into the passenger's seat, strapped the seat belt over her body, and sank back into the chair. The man smirked at Pearl and pressed his foot on the gas.

Discomfort swept over Pearl as she sat in silence. Her arms rested across her belly and her gaze stayed strictly forward on the road.

"You know," the man broke the silence, "it isn't safe for a young woman like you to be out here hopping into people's cars. You don't know who's out there."

"I have nothing to lose anymore, anyway." Pearl responded quietly, glancing out the window.

"Didn't your parents ever teach you not to trust anybody?"

"My parents are dead," Pearl replied rudely and abruptly, cutting the conversation short.

"Well, they weren't at one point, right?"

Pearl shot a quick glance at the man and raised an eyebrow. "What?"

"They had to have taught you at some point before they passed, right?" The man looked at Pearl, then back at the road.

Her eyebrows furrowed together, confused and annoyed. "Well, yeah."

"So, what are you doing, then?"

"What do you mean?" Pearl asked, shooting another glance at the man. "I already told you, my truck died, my phone died, and I need to get back to town. I would appreciate it if you would stop questioning me." Pearl looked away once again.

"That isn't any way to speak to someone who's doing you a favor, now is it?"

Pearl did not respond. Silence came over them for the moment.

"So, how did they go?" The man asked, breaking the silence.

"What?"

"How did they go? Your parents?" The man asked, his eyes glistening with a smug look on his face.

"I would rather not talk about this right now," Pearl said, still looking away.

"Sounds like that is not your only problem."

Pearl grew more annoyed and unsettled. "Sounds like you do not know when to stop talking."

"I am just trying to break the ice," he responded, laughing to himself.

"Well, you're about to make it crack, that's for sure." Pearl's breath grew short and her blood came to a boil. The truck became quiet once again as they continued their drive through the middle of nowhere.

After a few moments of awkward silence, the man felt encouraged to speak again. "Look, I'm sorry if I made you feel uncomfortable. That was not my intention. I just can't help but notice how dark your shadows are. I can see them seeping from your pores."

Pearl looked down at her arms and rubbed her skin, examining her pores up close. She looked at him with a puzzled look in her eyes. "What are you talking about?"

"You're trapped in the dark, aren't you? I felt it the second you sat down. I mean, your energy is just so low."

Her eyebrows creased as she glared at the man's big mouth. "Jeez, I did not realize I would be stepping into a car that was going to ridicule my entire life. You can let me out, now." Pearl spoke angrily, reaching for the door's handle while the car remained in motion. The man immediately locked it from the driver's side.

"Ridicule? I'm just trying to help you, little lady," he grinned. "What's your name?"

Pearl did not respond. She sat taller in her seat, lifting her back up and off the backrest, while picking her cuticles timidly in her lap. She kept her eyes locked on the road.

"Well, my name is Doc," the man spoke pridefully.

"What do you do, Doc?" Pearl asked, pretending to be interested despite the unsettling nerve of caution that slithered through her body. Her cuticles began to bleed.

"It is funny that you ask that, Pearl. I am a hypnotherapist. Have you ever done hypnosis?" He asked casually, glancing at Pearl.

Her heart just about stopped. Pearl turned her head toward the man, glaring deeply at his profile. "I never told you my name."

"You did not need to," Doc responded, keeping his eyes forward on the road.

Anxiety shot through her body like a scorching bullet. Uneasy and more tense than ever, Pearl continued to switch the conversation from herself back onto Doc, while reaching smoothly and slowly for her pepper spray at the bottom of her backpack. She kept her hand in her bag and waited for his next move.

"Hypnosis, huh? Do you—uh, swing a watch in front of someone's face and tell them to go to sleep, or something?" Pearl laughed nervously to herself, as if the man were crazy, joking, or both.

"Not exactly," he chuckled. "But you would think so, wouldn't you?" Doc paused, as he cleared his throat from phlegm, coughing a couple times. He continued, "No, I specialize with those who are struggling with depression and suicidal thoughts. Hence, why I know you are a victim, too."

Pearl paused for a moment, staring at him with unease. "You obviously just assume that I am," Pearl stated boldly.

"There is no reason to assume when I confidently can say that I just know." He tilted his head toward her and gave her a wink. The man's mysterious persona grew only more eerie and terrifying.

"Well, I—I—" Pearl stuttered.

"Would you ever consider hypnosis?" Doc asked curiously.

"I mean, I—I never have thought about hypnosis before, I—"

"Like you said, you have nothing to lose, right?"

"I mean, I—" Pearl stumbled and choked on her own words. Anxiety flooded through her veins faster than the toxic thoughts flooded her mind.

"How great would it be to be able to live the life you always have wanted? A life of happiness, a life full of light. Don't you want to live a life like that again, Pearl?" The man's eyes lit up and his smile grew even wider.

For a moment, Pearl's mind flashed back to the good times. The memories before her brother's death, and before her parents' numbness overruled them. Back then, she felt truly present and at peace with herself and the people around her. She hadn't needed to go to therapy every week, and suicide hadn't even been a passing thought. It was a time when she had felt genuinely free. Her lips curled slightly.

"So, what do you say, Pearl? Don't you want to live that life again?" Doc asked, still driving through the vast, untouched forest.

Pearl's mind returned to the present moment. "I mean, of course I would. Who wouldn't?"

"Why don't you, then?" He glanced over toward her.

She snickered. "If only it were that easy."

"Would you ever consider hypnosis?" He asked once more.

She thought for a second, her hand still gripped around the pepper spray. "I don't see why not, considering therapy has not been really helping me, anyway. Could be interesting."

A smile snaked across Doc's face. "I'm so glad you said that, Pearl." Doc began to press his foot slowly onto the breaks, until his car came to a complete stop. He shifted into park.

"What are you doing?" Pearl questioned. The hair on her skin rose tall and her stomach shot up into her throat. She pressed her back into the passenger's window. "Why are you stopping?"

"Are you ready?" His smile reached ear to ear and his pupils grew larger in size. Within an instant, Doc pulled out a woven, brown sack from the left side of his seat and with both hands, he engulfed Pearl's entire head into the bag, stealing her eyesight and breath in an instant. Pearl reacted fast and whipped out her pepper spray and pointed it toward Doc, spraying relentlessly in hopes of hitting him dead in the eyes. Luckily, she did. He let go of the bag and reached for his burning sockets.

Pearl ripped the bag off her head and slammed her thumb into the seatbelt's buckle, ripping it off her chest. She jolted the door's handle forcefully, finally unlocking it from her side, and slammed it open, running for her life. Blindly, Doc jumped out behind her, squinting his eyes in her direction, and ran after her. Despite his blurred vision, he ran fast, almost unnaturally fast, and he caught up to her almost immediately. He yanked her arm toward his chest, spinning her one hundred eighty degrees. Pearl's bag swung off her shoulder as she spun, facing the teary-eyed, deranged man. Her feet tripped over one another as she ran backwards, pulling Doc down into the ground with her. With dominance, Doc climbed on top, grabbed her flailing hands, pinned them down underneath his knees, and quickly slipped his hands around her neck. His cold fingers squeezed her tiny throat until suddenly, her whole world stopped with a single gasp.

# The Door to Her Subconscious Mind

1

Pearl's eyes slowly began to peel open, feeling as though they had been pressed together for eternity, opening to blackness, with only patches of light shining through. Between her teeth she felt a gag tied behind her head, constricting her cries. Immediately, she went into a panic. She tried jolting her arms and kicking her feet until she felt the intense pressure of zip ties holding all four of them down. Her head, too, was strapped back in place against the headrest behind her. She sat tied up, helpless, vulnerable, and with no control in a tattered, leather chair that wasn't the least bit comfortable.

Adrenaline rushed through her veins and poured all throughout her body. She felt fear beyond belief, and the anxiety of the unknown ate at her like acid on her skin. Apprehension overflowed every inch of her being and she shook uncontrollably with terror.

Suddenly, the woven brown bag lifted from Pearl's head, exposing her tired, worn-out eyes and her drooling, heavy jaw. Pearl's eyes opened wide as she immediately scoped out her surroundings.

In front of her was another leather seat identical to the one she was in, a small, wooden table with three legs between her and the other chair, and on top of the table sat a strange looking bracelet. Behind the table and chair stood a tall wall made of old, wood panels, and mounted along the wall were two oil lanterns that barely lit up the room. Between the hanging lights hung a Doctorate degree for psychology in a glass picture frame, awarded to Doc Stephens. Underneath, in another picture frame, displayed a hypnotherapy certificate granted to, lo and behold, Doc L. Stephens. Below that, other PhDs under his name. Pearl's eyes teared up once again, while her hands began to grip like a vulture's claw.

Doc made his way around Pearl, stopping right before her eyes. This time, he wore a white lab coat, and he held a rusted machete that had specks of blood splattered all over it in his right hand, and a half a cup of water in his left. He glared at Pearl with a wicked look in his eyes, took a sip of his water, then set the glass on the table between them. He licked his chapped lips, put his empty hand on his hip, and took a deep breath in and out.

"Wow, I am parched. You want a drink?" Doc asked her, as if there was no better time to be a good host.

Pearl glared back at him as if she were staring at the devil himself.

"Oh, my mistake," Doc chuckled to himself, bringing his hand over his stomach. "It would be kind of difficult for you to drink anything with this over your mouth."

He set the machete down, trotted his way back behind Pearl, untied the thick cloth that had been silencing her, and dropped it on the ground by her side. He walked back toward the other leather chair sitting across from Pearl, once again.

"Welcome to my office," Doc smiled.

"What have you done to me?" Pearl asked him as if it were more of a demand than a question. Tears began to race down her cheeks. "What are you going to do to me?"

"Why so tense? Make yourself at home, here." Doc began to twirl the machete in one hand as he grazed the top of the leather chair with the other.

"What the fuck do you want from me?" Pearl cringed.

"I think it would be more fun if we kept it a surprise. I love surprises. The anticipation of the unknown makes me all tingly inside, you know what I'm sayin'?"

"Please, I will do anything. Please just let me go, please," Pearl begged.

"That's funny, I am pretty sure you are the one that said you have nothing to lose, right?"

Pearl remained silent, closing her eyes tightly.

"You did also say that you were interested in hypnosis, correct?" Doc reminded her.

The only thing that came out of Pearl's mouth was the shortness of breath and the sad sobs that quivered from her lips. She was out of words.

"Pearl, I am here to help you! Maybe you cannot see that now, but eventually you will. You see, I have the power to change your entire life, just like you have been wishing for. That is what you have been wishing for, right?"

Pearl closed her eyes tighter since she could not look away from him. Tears squeezed through her eyelids, still pouring down her face. Doc walked up face to face with Pearl, so close that their noses were practically touching. He grabbed her right cheek with his left hand and pinched it like a baby's. His breath smelt rotten, as if he had not brushed his teeth in decades. It was simply nauseating.

"Right?" Doc asked once again.

"Please, I will do anything for you to let me go." Pearl opened her eyes wide and cried to Doc.

Doc stepped away from Pearl and sat in the other leather chair across from her. His eyes glanced at her, then down at his feet. He sat up, shifted his weight forward and rested his elbows onto his knees. He looked back up toward Pearl, smiled, so much so that he almost laughed, while he interlaced all ten fingers.

"You'll do anything?" He asked her, grinding his teeth together.

"Yes, I'll do anything."

"Pearl," Doc stated. He stood up and paced around the chair yet again, keeping his fingers interlaced. "You have no idea who I am, do you?"

Pearl stared at him blankly, petrified.

"Do you know who I am?"

"No," Pearl responded, thinking she should comply if she wanted to stay alive.

Doc chuckled to himself, until his smile faded into a deep scowl. His voice grew lower. "Do you see these plaques?" He asked, as he pointed at his framed achievements.

"Yes."

Doc began to pace once again. "I am Doctor Doc Lance Stephens. I am a globally known doctor, psychologist, scientist, whatever you want to call me—I have done it all. I have worked my ass off to get to where I am now, and I have trained my mind to be the absolute best. I have always known from a young age that I had a gift, a gift that was so powerful that I had no choice but to share it with the world... to people who suffer with the darkest of demons, people that are so sad that they are willing to die. People like you." He paused, staring at Pearl dead in her eyes, "I have more power in my fucking fingertip than you do in your entire body!" He shouted at her, reaching his pinky out so she could see it. His fuming face relaxed and transformed back into a soft, sincere smile. He really believed that he was an all and mighty power, as if he were a god. He seemed to be extremely prideful and confident with himself, but one thing was certain: he was out of his mind. More tears fell from her face, once again.

"Please, I—I have to get out of here. I don't belong here. I—I—I—" she stuttered, pleading to Doc to spare her.

Doc stepped closer to Pearl. He picked up the bracelet resting on top of the table and buried it in his coat pocket. Making himself comfortable, he sat on top of the table with his legs spread open wide. He leaned in like he was telling her a secret.

"How would you like to enter a place I like to call The Maze?" He whispered, grinning widely.

Pearl frowned and her breath grew even shorter.

"Hm?" Doc muttered.

"The Maze? What is it? Where is it?" Pearl asked in a panic while her breath grew even heavier.

"The Maze is that tiny place inside here," he stated enthusiastically, as he pointed at Pearl's temple. "It's that dark place in here that is holding you back from the life you could be living!"

Pearl stared back at him like a deer caught in headlights.

"Look, the reason you are depressed is because of this thing in here, right? Your world has become so dark that your vision can no longer see clearly. You have become so caught up in this sob story you have been telling yourself for who knows how long that ultimately, you're doing it to yourself!" Doc stood up and flailed his arms in the air, like 'why doesn't anyone understand what the fuck I am talking about?'

Pearl remained silent, barely involuntarily breathing. Doc came close to her face.

"I can give you access to that part of your mind," he muttered, his lips trembling. "I have the power to grant you permission."

The tears couldn't stop. She began to think about how shitty her last few moments were, how the news would get out, if the news would even get out, if anyone would care, or if anyone would even notice. These thoughts made her weep even more.

"You can change your reality, Pearl. If you are strong enough to make it out." Doc persisted, exceptionally sure with himself. "Don't you want to do that?"

"Please, please just let me go," she begged, while shaking her locked head slightly back and forth, sweating profusely underneath the straps.

"Well, fortunately for you, Pearl, I am offering my services to you today at no charge. You should be rather honored to receive my services." He stood back onto his feet, reached into his coat pocket, and pulled out the bracelet that she noticed sitting on the table beforehand. He tied the bracelet on her right wrist, just behind the zip tie. "You'll need to take this with you."

Pearl shifted her gaze down toward the bracelet. Since her head remained tied back, she could not get a good look, but she did notice that it was a measly piece of white string with multiple chain links and a single, pink pearl hanging from it. She looked back at him wide eyed, dropped her jaw, and let out a mighty scream.

"Let me go!!! Please, let me g—"

"You best not lose that bracelet. You will never forgive yourself if you do."

"Wha—what is this!?"

"You will find out soon enough. But like I said, do not lose it. If you do, you will spend the rest of your existence in The Maze. Personally, I think that would be kind of fun. The light just gets so boring sometimes, you know?" Doc paused, glaring deeply into Pearl's eyes. "Soon, you will understand. But for now, all you have to do is relax."

He sat back down into the other leather chair, leaned back into his seat, and flashed Pearl a smile.

"Take a deep breath in through your nose with me." Doc breathed in, filling his lungs with air, then sighed with a deeper exhale out. However, Pearl did not join him. She remained silent, in fact she consciously held her breath. This infuriated him.

"Pearl," he stated, with anger creeping up his throat. "It would be in your best interest for you to do what I say. See, this is a fun game we are playing. Right now, it's your turn. You can either choose to listen to what I tell you, or you can play the hard way. And don't be fooled, I love playing the hard way."

Pearl stared at him, repulsed.

"Oh, are you wondering about how hard the hard way is played? Well, do you see these marks?" Doc pointed at the blood on his machete. "These are the stains of people like yourself who wanted to play the hard way. They even sat in that very chair you're sitting in, and they believed noncompliance was the best way to go. You know where they are now, Pearl?"

Pearl continued to stare into his warped eyes, while more tears rolled down her cheeks.

He rubbed the corner of the blade slowly and steadily. "Let's just say that those patients have been released. A slow, painful, gut-wrenching release. They never even had a chance to step foot into The Maze, anyway, so maybe it was for the best. There would have been no way for them to make it out, for they were clearly too weak. But you, Pearl, you do have a chance. I can see it in you. You must trust me." Doc smiled widely and his eyes looked hopefully into hers. "And if you don't, I will slice you open and drain your insides like a cow at a slaughterhouse, while I watch you squirm in your seat, screaming for help in anguish. Even though—" he paused, laughing to himself, "—even though we are miles and miles away from anyone ever hearing you. Which way do you want to play? The easy way, or the hard way?"

Pearl clenched her eyes shut, gritted her teeth, and let out another desperate cry. She peeled her distraught eyes back open and looked back into Doc's. "I'll do it. I'll go. I'll go to The Maze." She cried desperately.

Doc smiled softly with his eyes locked on Pearl's. "Take a deep breath in with me now." Doc demanded, giving her one more chance as he led with a full breath in. She followed with an inhale.

"Deep breath out."

She exhaled with him.

"Another breath. Inhale." Doc breathed in through his nose to demonstrate.

Pearl copied.

"Sigh it out."

She did.

"Continue this breath, long inhales through your nose, and longer exhales out of your mouth." Doc padded behind his empty chair and picked up a bronze gong that appeared a bit bigger than the size of his head, and a small mallet that came with it. He set it down softly on the table between them. Pearl continued her voluntary breath, trying to make it as calm and as believable as possible, when she really wanted to explode on the inside.

"Continue your breath and keep your eyes on mine," he ordered.

She took another breath in and another breath out, keeping her traumatized eyes on his.

They continued this conscious flow of inhales and exhales for about five minutes, until suddenly, Doc struck the gong with the mallet for the first time for Pearl. The vibration shot through her ears, her body, her mind, so much so that her eyes clamped closed.

"Open your eyes, Pearl. Look into my eyes." He instructed, as his pupils began to fill his entire sockets until both eyes were completely black. She opened hers once again, and the sight of his flooded black eyes made her fearful even more. Unnervingly, her conscious breath came to a stop. He appeared out of this world, as if he were not even human. She could not believe her eyes.

"Take another breath in, Pearl."

She couldn't. The sight of his evil eyes was too much to take in.

"Breathe, now, or I'll cut you open and turn your insides to outsides." He demanded, with fury in his voice.

Pearl blinked away the tears, looked deep into his eyes once again, and with the best of her abilities, she took another mighty breath in.

A few more moments later, with their eyes still locked onto one another, Doc struck the gong for the second time, vibrating the two of them and everything in the room. For Pearl, this second vibration pierced its way through the veil of her consciousness. Her attention became captured, and her awareness tuned deeper into her breath than ever before, without her even knowing.

Doc's smile grew more unsettling. Suddenly, with his hypnotizing eyes captivating hers, he spoke aloud. "You have permission to access your subconscious mind. You will now enter The Maze." Suddenly, for the third and final time, he struck the gong with the mallet, shocking Pearl's system. In an instant, she gasped for a breath in like it was the first breath she had ever taken, until she let out a lifeless sigh. Her eyes fell closed, instantly. In that one breath, she had sunken deep into the pit of her mind. Her body became nothing more than a pile of flesh and bones.

The lids of her eyes drooped and were lifeless. Her consciousness floated away and just like that; reality stood behind her. Pearl had entered a place she could have never thought to imagine. She was not necessarily gone, for her soul was still active, alive, and present. She had just stepped foot into a whole other dimension. She fell under.

2

In this place in her mind, Pearl found herself physically standing alone in the center of a white abyss. This abyss had no walls, no floor, and no ground. Yet, in this dimension, she stood free from the leather chair, gag, and zip ties. In the physical world, on the other hand, her body remained sunken in the leather chair, arms and ankles still tied and eyes still shut.

Pearl spun her body around, looking down past her feet and up at the never ending white sky above. Her hands roamed over her arms, legs, stomach, and chest, feeling her body to see if she were really standing there, or if she were standing in a dream. Her heart fluttered exponentially, and her breath ran short. Suddenly, like a surround-sound speaker, Doc's voice echoed throughout.

"Listen to me closely, Pearl," Doc spoke slowly and clearly. "The subconscious mind works with images. So, for you to connect to your subconscious mind, you must tap into your imagination. I want you to visualize a large door standing right in front of you. This door is made of wood. It is painted cherry red and it has a golden doorknob. Visualize every detail and focus. Breathe in."

Pearl's subconscious mind visualized a door right before her eyes in the white void. Suddenly, a red, wooden door with four panels and a golden handle physically appeared in front of her. The two of them, Pearl and the red door, stood before each other, as her body that remained in the physical world inhaled subconsciously.

"Full breath out."

Her hypnotized body exhaled. Yet, this exhalation echoed in the abyss, and she heard her own breath exhaling out from the human realm. "What's happening to me?" Pearl spoke aloud to herself in the abyss.

"Now, imagine this door opening before your eyes. As it opens, you visualize a stream of energy flowing through. With every inhalation, you see this energy flow into the door," Doc continued explaining.

In the physical world, her body took another deep breath in. Pearl began to panic, as she listened to her mind and her body obeying Doc from the outside world.

"Stop! Don't listen to him!" Pearl yelled out loud to herself, hoping her physical being would hear her and listen to her cries.

"And with every breath that leaves your body, you watch the stream of energy flow out the door, leaving calmly and slowly," Doc continued, his voice like an intercom.

Her body sighed. Just then, the ebb and flow of a white energy, like a subtle wind, began to visibly flow in and out through the door.

"What color do you see this energy as? Think to yourself."

Suddenly, the energy that flowed through the door transformed into a dark, hellish shade. Like a black, ferocious wave underneath a heavy, powerful storm, it rushed in and out of the door.

"Stop! Don't listen to what he is saying! It's all a trap!" Pearl screamed in the white void, but no matter how loudly she cried, her physical body was deaf to her commands, as it persisted to breathe when told.

"Take another full breath in through your nose," Doc whispered.

Her lungs inhaled.

"Exhale."

She subconsciously did as she was told.

"As you continue to focus on this flow of energy within, the power of your breath, you begin to visualize yourself standing in front of the cherry red, wooden door. Do you see yourself in front of the door? If so, tap the leather with your thumb three times."

In the physical world, Pearl's body subconsciously lifted its thumb and tapped the chair three times.

"Excellent. Begin to make your way toward this door. Walk through the door. May you become one with this wave of energy that is flowing through. May you flow through it and to the other side."

The red door standing before her began to open wider, and the black, ferocious wave grew more agitated. Pearl swallowed the dry lump in her throat and took a deep breath in, and a deeper breath out, this time on her own. She looked to her left, to her right, and over her shoulder. Nothing stood in sight except for the single, red door.

"I have no choice," she whispered to herself as a tear rolled down her cheek. So, she made the conscious decision in her subconscious to go through. Step by step, through the red door, she made her way through the gush of energy. There she stood, in the center of the doorway, her hair blowing back and forth with the black, flowing wave, like she was standing in a gust of wind. With a few more small steps, Pearl found herself walking through the door, making her way through to the other side, and in that instant, the door slammed behind her. Just like that, she had entered The Maze within her mind.

Everything went black.

# Psych Ward

1

"You abducted her," Tom claimed, rather than asking.

"Pfft," Doc snorted, "I told you that she wanted to try hypnosis. So, we did just that."

"It's hard to believe someone who willingly wants to try something new has to get their head shoved into a bag and suffocated to do so. Wouldn't you agree, Doctor?"

Doc remained silent, but with a smile plastered from cheek to cheek. Randy and Allan glanced at one another, raised an eyebrow, and then peered back in Doc's direction.

Tom continued the interview. "How did you know her name? Were you stalking her before you abducted her?"

"I did not stalk her."

"Then how did you know her name without her even telling you?"

"I guess you could say I just have a knack for knowing things. You could call it a sixth sense." He laughed to himself.

"Do you have psychic abilities?" Allan chimed in from behind the camera. He could not resist asking.

"Ha," Doc chuckled, "I don't know if I would call them 'psychic abilities.' I guess that's for me to know, and for you to wonder."

Allan and Randy glanced at each other, cringing.

"So, what happened next? You did your work. You put her under, just like that?" Tom asked him.

"Just like that," Doc responded.

"I have a question," Allan projected once again. "There is a lot of talk about hypnosis being a sham. Would you—"

"—If it was a sham, do you think you three would be here, interviewing me today?" Doc interrupted, while staring through Allan.

"I suppose not," Allan said. "But is it true that hypnosis only works if you are mentally weak?"

Doc continued to glare at Allan. His smile faded into a frown and his pupils filled the color in his eyes. He grew visibly angry. "I'm not quite sure, Allan. Do you want to try it out?"

"Let's just get back to the story," Tom intervened, trying to distract from the tension. "So, you opened the door to her subconscious mind..."

"That's correct."

"What did you do next?"

"I did not do anything after that. What happened next was up to Pearl. All I did was give her access to that space within her mind. My work was complete. It was her that did the rest of the work."

# THE MAZE

1

Pearl's eyes shot open wide. First, she instinctively looked her body up and down. She found herself wearing the same clothing she had put on that morning. When she gazed down at her feet, she noticed she was standing on a dirt path that stretched out long in front of her. She lifted her head, squinted her eyes, and scanned her surroundings. She stood in the middle of a forest, unlike any other forest she had seen. All around her stood hundreds of thousands of lush birch trees that grew about fifty feet tall. Above her, she could see patches of grey clouds through the infinite number of branches and flourishing, green leaves. Every direction looked the same except for the single, dirt trail that stretched far out before her eyes. Even the wind brushing against her skin felt cold and crisp. This place felt too real. *Where the fuck am I?* She thought to herself.

Panic began to overflow throughout her being. She immediately remembered Doc, being abducted, and forcibly put into a trance of hypnosis. As she recollected her thoughts, she remembered the bracelet Doc gave her prior. She shifted her gaze down toward her wrist, and there it rested, lo and behold, the measly bracelet.

"What the fuck? No—no—this can't be happening," Pearl cried aloud. She began to hyperventilate, as the rhythm of her heart pounded harder and her breath grew even faster. Pearl spun around fiercely in all different directions. Her eyes filled with tears and she screamed at the top of her lungs. "Get me out of this place! I do not want to be here! I don't belong here!"

Pearl dropped down to her knees, curled her spine over, and hid her face in the palms of her hands. Her eyes flooded as she began to bawl. "This isn't happening. This can't be happening." For a moment, she believed she had gone insane. She rocked back and forth, wrapped her hands around the sides of her head, and submitted to the anxiety that crept throughout her blood and bones.

Suddenly, after a few minutes of cognitive dissonance, thunder pounded throughout the sky, vibrating the earth floor and the entire forest before her. Pearl lifted her head and looked up. With her eyes red and wide, a drop of rain landed in the center of her forehead and dripped down the bridge of her nose. She wiped the droplet and took a few shallow breaths. She pressed herself up and off the ground and took off sprinting down the dirt path before her, in the hopes of finding her way out.

Pearl ran wild in the outskirts of her mind. Her feet ran faster than the thoughts that raced through her mind, as she made her way through the trees and further into the unknown. She ran with fear, uncertainty, and worry, and she felt as if she were choking on her own stomach. The sensation of a deep, dark hole drilled through her insides, and the feeling of the world closed in. She felt terrified.

2

After what felt like hours of running, while simultaneously swimming in an ocean of cruel emotions, the dirt path began to change shape. When Pearl came around the bend, she noticed the trail went straight into a wall of birch trees, however, it did not end. In fact, it morphed into dirt stairs that traveled deep down into the ground below. She stopped and stared for a moment, confused and uneasy as to where this path was leading her to. With stealth, she prowled closer.

She eventually made her way to the top of the stairs. She peaked her head over and looked down into the ground, following the steps one by one with her eyes. Just like her breath, her mind raced a million miles per hour as she contemplated her next move. *Should I turn back around? Should I walk down there?* She wondered. As the rain began to fall harder and heavier, she felt as if she had no choice but to follow the trail down into the earth floor.

One foot after the other, she crept down the steps with caution. She walked down thirteen steps until she finally made it to another flat, dirt path once again.

At the bottom of the steps, she noticed the path continued to lead her into a narrow, dirt tunnel. The only light that traveled through this tunnel came from the natural light shining from the top of the staircase. But at the end of the dirt tunnel, she noticed another enormous red door with a bronze doorknob standing about fifteen feet ahead. Her body froze like a statue. As she observed the door from the last step, the rain began to come down even harder. Pearl made her way toward the eerie, unfamiliar door at the end of the tunnel. She lifted her hand up and grazed her fingertips against the door's surface, feeling the wood from top to bottom, until she grabbed hold of the knob. Before she turned it, she paused for a moment. The hair on her arms rose tall, and she felt a sensation of unease creep through her whole body. She took a deep breath in, and even a deeper breath out. Then, without thinking twice, she turned the doorknob and pushed the door open.

3

The door swung open wide and welcomed her to nothing but darkness. It was so dark that it didn't matter if Pearl's eyes were opened or closed. She tried to swallow despite her dry mouth, and her heart pounding practically out of her chest. She took one step through the door, followed by another. She moved with attentiveness, her body tense, and her breath short.

As she took a few more steps inside, the door slammed shut behind her. She immediately turned around and ran to where the red door once stood, but it had vanished in thin air and was no longer present. Instead, a cement wall took its place.

"What the fuck? No! Open the door! Please!" Pearl screamed, banging her hands against the cement wall. She jolted her body into the wall, as if with force, the door would magically appear once again. Unfortunately, she had entered a place that took more than begging for mercy to get out of, and her only option was to move forward.

Pearl shoved her face into the wall, and she unleashed a hysterical cry. Petrified tears washed down her face and dripped off her chin. She sobbed, while clenching her eyes shut and recollecting her breath. Fear crept throughout her body, and she became absorbed with the discomfort of the unimaginable unknown. Suddenly, in the midst of her tears, a few small lights illuminated behind her, slowly lighting up the darkness. She turned around and opened her eyes.

The room she had entered looked as if it were a windowless hallway that stretched long and narrow in front of her. The walls were made of cement and painted blood red, and they had cracks cut deep throughout them. The walls rose tall, there was no ceiling in sight. Down the hall hung a few, flickering lightbulbs from extension cords, swaying ever so slightly back and forth. The bulbs flickered uncontrollably, barely providing enough light for Pearl to see clearly. The air in this hallway felt thick, heavy, and cold, and it had a repulsive smell like watered-down sewage. In the distance, she heard a faint dripping noise that sounded like a loose faucet. Adrenaline shot through Pearl's veins, and she felt nothing less than terrified.

Suddenly, in the darkness down the hall, something caught her eye. Out of the shadows emerged a silhouette of what appeared to be a man, yet this man was no human. He appeared to be otherworldly and infernal. He stood immensely tall, around seven feet. He had an extremely long, slender face, and his cheeks sunk deep into his skull. His skin appeared pasty white, practically grey, and he had large, dark circles underneath his eyes. His eyes, on the other hand, were filled with nothing but white, yet, in the center of each eye was a tiny, black, pinhole-like dot. His nose looked like a vulture's beak, and he had a smile that drooped down over his protruding, pointy chin. His shoulders were small and fragile, and he had a large hump resting on his back. He carried his arms like a dinosaur; his elbows bent and his hands hanging downward, close beside his torso. His body was draped with a long, black cloak and the top of his head was covered by a large, dark hood.

"Welcome, Pearl," The creature spoke with a deep, scratchy voice.

Pearl stood still for a moment. Her chest began to noticeably rise and fall as her breath flowed rapidly in and out. The hair on her body rose tall toward the sky and anxiety seeped from her pores.

"Who are you and where the hell am I?" She spoke with angst.

The creature continued to smirk in a gut-wrenching manner. "You must not worry about who I am. I am here to welcome you to The Maze."

Pearl looked at him, unsettled, with an eyebrow raised high. "What are you talking about? What do you mean Th—The Maze?" She stuttered.

"The Maze. You have entered The Maze within your mind. That space of horrendous darkness you live in comfortably, yet miserably, every single day of your life. That place in your head that tears you down every second of the day. The prison where you are locked up as a slave to your own thoughts, giving them full permission to eat you alive from the inside out. You are a victim of your own reality and you crave for your fire of life to burn out. You are blind to your meaning of existence and you experience every moment on the very surface of life. However, may this be your first experience within your latent mind. Your subconscious state of being. Some call it another dimension. Others call it a different realm." The man paused. A smile crept across his face and he chuckled, "But many people call it hell."

Pearl's eyes flooded with tears of terror once again, her breath accelerating and her pulse pounding. She took a few steps back behind her and pressed her back into the cement wall.

"Please, sir. You have to get me out of here. I did not mean to come here. This was an accident. I do not belong in this place."

The man laughed again. "Not a single person accidentally enters The Maze. Nobody is here by mistake. It does not matter what you came here for, or what traumas you carry with you. Everyone and everything that is here suffers like you. But, despite our differences, we all end up in this same place; this place of depression, sadness, and fear. This place of utmost darkness is a real, living hell. You are meant to be here, Pearl, and you must find your way out alive, ultimately peeling back the layers of trauma that you've allowed to grow over you for all of these years." He paused, blinking his eyes together tightly. He opened them again, but, this time, they were engulfed by blackness. He continued with a smile, "If you do not, you will become forever trapped like the rest of us, living in the dark for eternity."

Pearl hugged her body tight, gripping her opposite elbows. Tears rolled down her face and dripped down her jaw. Her lips quivered, and she whispered to herself, "This cannot be real. This is not happening. This is all in my head."

"You are correct. This is all in your head. Now, you will be forced to face your depressed, suppressed, and utmost intense emotions that keep you from stepping into your ultimate truth. You decide who is in charge. You, or your thoughts. May you find your strength, find your Self, and conquer. Good luck, you will need it my friend."

And just like that, with the blink of an eye, the unholy man disappeared.

Pearl stood there with her back pressed into the wall, alone and afraid. Her breath was loud, and her chest puffed up and down as she fretted. Her skin crawled all over her body as she cringed with fear. Every muscle constricted with tension, and not one part of her being felt settled. Not one bit.

She quickly turned her body back around and clenched her fists. She lifted her arms up and began pounding the cement wall for the second time, letting out a terrified screech for help. "Get me the fuck out of this place! Please!!" As she pounded her fists, she noticed the flimsy bracelet that Doc tied around her wrist once again. She relaxed her fists, as she shifted her focus onto the bracelet. She began to count the number of chain links alongside the shiny, pink pearl that it carried, counting a total of ten chain links around her wrist. She wondered, for a moment, as to why Doc had given her this piece of jewelry. Pearl remembered his voice of warning and his encouragement for the journey she was about to experience, and how vital this bracelet would be as she went. She grazed her fingertips around each chain link, observing the details up close. She stood there, swaying slightly back and forth, thinking to herself. Then, she lifted her chin, wiped her eyes clean, rolled her shoulders down her spine, and took a full breath in. Unsure as to what her next move would be, she turned around and reluctantly walked forward into The Maze.


4


One step after another, she moved stealthily on her tiptoes down the long, blood red hallway. She prowled forward in the center of the hall, mindfully keeping her body away from the walls beside her. Her body shivered and shook, and the beat of her heart accelerated with every step she took. As Pearl crept deeper into The Maze, she noticed the hall turn left at a corner up ahead. She continued forward.

What felt like the longest walk of her life, Pearl finally approached the end of the hall before it led her around the corner. Quietly, she peaked her eyes past the wall, glimpsing toward the new unmarked territory. In this hall, she noticed the red paint on the walls and how it stretched abnormally long and far like the first. Just like before, it had only a few, flickering lightbulbs that hung from the never-ending ceiling. Pearl held her breath, squeezed her eyes shut for a moment, working up the courage to continue forward. She opened her eyes, peeked around the corner once more, until she stepped forward with caution, making her way further into The Maze.

She skulked through the red halls and thick, dense air until the hallway eventually led her to a dead end. Yet, as she approached the end of the hall, she noticed five different doors standing tall in the hall before her.

The first door she noticed appeared off-white and looked as if it had previously caught fire. The corners of this door were burnt to a crisp, as though the door had managed to survive a severe fire. However, despite its catastrophe, its handle appeared untouched and polished.

The second door had a round, wooden door frame with brown trim. The door was a dirty-brown color constructed of old wood, and it had cracks that split all over it. She could see splints of wood poking off the door, and even chips of wood gradually rotting away. This door had no doorknob, in fact it had nothing but an empty hole where one would expect it to be.

The next door she noticed stood tall and narrow. The door appeared to be painted a bright, orange color, and it had beautiful, carved wood-work all over of symbolic and creative designs.

The following door was painted a deep, dark red color, almost blending in with the hallway itself. Near the top center of the door, was a small, rect-angular window with three metal poles vertically sticking through, like an old dungeon cell. Although the window contained no glass, all that was seen through the poles appeared to be only pitch darkness.

Lastly, at the end of the hall, Pearl saw a beautiful door made of mahogany with a brass lion head door knocker in the top center of the door, and a brass doorknob below. "What is this? Where the fuck am I?" Pearl spoke quietly to herself.

She stepped up to each door and examined them even closer. *Am I supposed to go through one of them? Which one do I choose? Do they mean something?* She pondered. As she thought to herself, she quickly glanced over her shoulder. Nothing had changed behind her, so she turned her attention back toward the doors standing before her.

As she examined their drastic differences, she lifted her right hand up in front of her and began to graze each of the doors with the tips of her fingers. She felt them as if they were from a whole new world.

Suddenly, around the corner behind her, she heard light, quick footsteps running toward her. Pearl quickly turned her body around, peering down toward the other end of the hall. Her eyes shot open wide.

At the end of the hall, there stood a young boy, around the age of nine or ten. He wore a faded black, button-down shirt with short sleeves rolled up his small biceps. His skin appeared sickly white, with fresh, bloody cuts and yellow bruises all over. He had a wide head, and rosy, red cheeks, a long, pointed nose, and eyes that resembled those of a goat. His pupils appeared to be rectangles of black, and his eyes looked cracked with blood. He had a grin painted across his face, exposing hundreds of tiny, baby teeth growing out of his gums. His teeth were rotting brown, some drilled with holes and others chipped to jagged points.

Pearl believed her eyes to be deceiving her. With hesitation, she took a step back and found herself pressed into the mahogany door with lion head door knocker. Her chest started to rise and fall rapidly with anticipation. She could barely catch a breath, as terror swept over her once again.

"Hello?" Pearl asked, raising one eyebrow.

The boy remained silent, yet his smile grew wider. He took a few steps forward toward Pearl.

"Who are you?" Pearl asked. Her shoulders raised high up toward her ears and her hands gripped onto the door behind her.

The boy continued walking in her direction, as he began to laugh out loud.

"What are you doing here?"

He stopped in his place and stared, this time, his smile growing up to his temples, his hundreds of teeth turning into thousands.

"Do you want to play?" The child asked Pearl with a scratch in his voice. Before Pearl had a chance to respond, the boy made a run for it, sprinting as fast as he could toward Pearl. Within an instant, adrenaline shot through Pearl's veins and anxiety overrode her entire being once again. She whipped her body around back toward the mahogany door, gripped the brass knob with both hands, and turned it with force, pushing the door open in front of her. She jolted her body through and slammed it closed behind her. Amid all the chaos, she had officially entered the first door of The Maze.

# Door #1
# I Am Alone

1

She stood face to face with the back of the door. She kept her gaze down toward her toes and her shoulders practically glued to her earlobes. Pearl took a relieving breath in and out, thankful she escaped the presence of the young, gut-wrenching boy with a thousand teeth. *Who was that? What was that?* She cringed as she wondered. Amid her curiosity, a gust of wind blew against the back of her head, blowing her hair over her eyes and into her mouth. She turned around instantly. Suddenly, a sensation of unease, discomfort, and anxiety sped through her body. Pearl gasped for a breath and her eyes opened wider than ever before.

This door appeared to be a portal to a whole other world. On the other side of the door was an entry to a vast, overgrown island in the middle of the ocean. Before her eyes stretched a long, white, sandy beach. To the left of the beach grew a mighty, overflowing jungle; nothing but green for as far as her eyes could see. On the right side of the beach, the rough waves crashed onto the shore abruptly, bringing seashells and seaweed along with them. Meanwhile, the clear sky and hot, red sun beat down on Pearl. She stood alone and full of fear, her jaw dropped and her lungs clasping onto her breath. She placed her hand over her eyes for shade and squinted, hoping her eyes were fooling. Alas, her eyes perceived clearly, and not one person stood in sight.

Pearl backed up, confused and hardly believing, as she tried to make sense of the senseless situation. She took a step back, thinking she would back up into the mahogany door. Rather, as she stepped back, she tripped over a large rock and stumbled. Immediately, she whipped her body around to where the door once stood, coming to find that it had vanished into thin air. Pearl grew more confused, uneasy, and distraught than ever.

"What the fuck? Where's the door?" She spoke out loud, trying to catch her rapid breath. Pearl spun her whole body in circles as she frantically searched for the missing door. However, nothing stood in the door's place except for the white, untouched sand, rocks of all different shapes and sizes, and seemingly perfect seashells strewn beautifully underneath the rays of the sun. "No fucking way this is happening to me."

The beat of her heart pounded against the inside of her chest. Her breath became audible, as she huffed and puffed with adrenaline pumping through her veins like an IV injection. Every hair on her body stood up, and her sweat felt icy cold despite her boiling insides. Terror chilled her being.

Out of thoughtless effort, her feet began sprinting down the beach. Her mind raced along with her, shouting a thousand thoughts a minute. *Where am I? How did I get here? How the fuck do I get out of here? Where is the door? It was just there. How else would I have gotten here? Where is anybody? Where am I? What the fuck is happening? What do I do? Where do I go?*

Just like that, the voices of her corrupt mind became the center of attention. Her mind chattered so loudly with the thoughts of 'whys' and 'hows' that she was deaf to the truth of what The Maze was trying to tell her. She became engulfed in fear, and panic dominated both her body and her mind.

After a few short minutes, she came to a halt in the middle of the beach. She spun in circles once again, gasping for breath. Pearl dropped down to her knees, as the rhythm of her heart and the overflowing anxiety became too much. She buried her head into the palms of her hands as she folded her torso over her thighs. Her whole body trembled and convulsed as the tears rushed down the sides of her face. The only presence in this moment was the storm of perturbation and sheer terror.

Eventually, Pearl blinked the tears away as she recollected her breath. She began to peel herself back up and away from the tops of her legs. Her breath involuntarily flowed as she found her face drenched in tears and sweat, and her vision blurred from pressing her eyes too deep into her palms. Her nose dripped, and her quivering mouth fell slightly open. She hugged her biceps into her ribs as every part of her body pulsed. She slowly looked out in front of her as her eyes became clearer, taking in the view another time.

Finally, Pearl pushed herself up and off the sand and back onto her feet. As she grabbed her opposite arms, her fingers still rattling, she stopped and observed. She raised a hand to her forehead to shade her eyes once again as she scanned the island from right to left, turning her body in another full circle. *I have to get the fuck out of this place,* she thought to herself. So, she went on.

2

She walked down the beach for what felt like forever, looking nonstop for any sign of life that she could find. Yet, the only signs of life she could see were the birds that sat on the tops of branches watching down at her, a few small crabs running from the top of the sand down to the water below, and insects of all shapes and sizes crawling around her. As Pearl wandered, she continuously looked back behind her to see if anyone would appear, yet she found herself disappointed with every glance she took.

She believed to be alone; alone on the island, alone in the world, and alone with only the thoughts that echoed in her mind. She would constantly overthink and tell herself made-up stories that only she would believe in. Eventually, these deceiving tales became her reality, as she simply manifested the worst of the world without even knowing it. She had no awareness of the game she had signed herself up for, no awareness of the matrix, and she found herself imprisoned in her mind, unknowingly torturing herself on a daily basis. She convinced herself to be a victim of the world. Although the deck of cards she was dealt were not the best, she still held them in her hand, with control she did not know she had. *Why me? Why me?* She always asked herself. She pondered this question as she skulked along the water.

Suddenly, at the end of the beach, about five hundred yards away, she began to make shape of what looked like a figure walking toward her. At first, she could barely make out what it was. All she saw was what looked to be a blurred silhouette of a human body moseying from afar. She squinted her eyes to get a closer look.

"Hey!" She screamed at the top of her lungs, waving both hands up in the air.

The figure continued to shamble on as if it did not notice Pearl.

"Hello!! Can you hear me!?" She yelled again, this time louder than before, as she continued to wave her hands back and forth.

The silhouette stopped in its place and looked in Pearl's direction.

Pearl started running to the other side of the beach. "Please help me! Please!" She yelled louder. Her eyes continued to peer at the figure as she picked up the pace. Suddenly, the figure became clear. Pearl went from running full speed, to lightly jogging, to walking, until finally, a complete stop. Her eyes grew wider with alarm and disbelief.

At the end of the beach, she noticed the figure stood small, like a child, and he had short, black hair on his head and black attire covering his small body. There he stood, the boy with a thousand teeth, motionless in his stance, yet staring back at Pearl.

The beat of Pearl's heart began to race faster once again. She released her hands back down by her sides and took a step back behind her, her eyes still locked on the boy. She felt paralyzed with fear.

Instantly, the boy began to race toward Pearl.

"Oh, fuck," Pearl's pupils swallowed both of her irises. Immediately, she ran faster than she had ever before. She huffed and puffed as her breath ran out faster than her feet could cover ground, yet, she knew she was in desperate need of getting off the beach. After a glance behind her and up ahead, she jolted up the rocks that sat alongside the sand, and threw her body into the depths of the lively jungle, entering a whole other world.

Pearl ran through massive, green palm leaves, elephant ears, and monsteras, shoving them out of her way as she darted through. She sprinted uphill through the jungle as fast as she could, dodging tree trunks and hurdling over rocks that sat in her way. She had no idea where she would end up. All she knew was that she needed to run away and run away fast.

Frantic for breath, Pearl raced through the forest for what felt like a lifetime, as she continuously shot glances over her shoulders to see if the otherworldly boy followed behind. Eventually, she turned back once more and found herself alone amongst the jungle life. The boy had vanished.

Pearl's footsteps slowed and eventually came to a stop. She stood there, huffing and puffing for breath underneath the canopy of trees, lost in the outskirts of her mind. Looking in every direction around her, she searched for the boy with a thousand teeth. Her eyebrows creased with confusion and worry as her mind finally caught up with her breath. *This cannot be happening; this is not real. I am in a dream. I must be dreaming.* But despite what she told herself, her senses remained true. This place felt too real to be a dream. In fact, she denied the familiar feeling she had felt the moment she had entered The Maze, the feeling of darkness that clouded her mind every day she lived. Except this time, rather than the darkness traveling through her, she became one that traveled within the darkness. Alone and lost on this deserted island, she stood. Pearl felt that the only thing she could do was to let out the most grieving, devastated screech she could make.

*"Rrrraaaaaaaaaaaaahhhhhhhh!!!* Why did you do this to me!? Let me go!!!" She cried at the top of her lungs, her chin pointed up toward the sky and her arms out by her sides. Her hands tore at the air, and then

clenched into defeated fists. Her heart hammered against her chest and overwhelming thoughts bounced from each side of her skull. She could not take it. *I am alone. I am alone on a deserted island. I can't get out of here. I am going to die. This is it. This is the end. This is the end. This is the end.* Her manipulative thoughts spoke without sympathy.

3

Pearl wandered through the jungle for three days and two nights. During the day, she scavenged for food in hopes to get her by. On the first day, she came across a bush of red berries that she deemed to be trusting. That lasted until her whole body broke out in hives from the moment she swallowed one. Later that day, she spent time gathering wood in hopes to build a fire for the night. She was pleased to discover a large, fallen tree, providing her more than enough wood for a fire, until she realized starting a fire would be just another obstacle she had to face. She tried her best, rubbing rocks and sticks together, but without flint, a match, or a lighter, she could only get so far.

The next day, she found herself back on the white sand, scavenging the tidepools in hopes to suffice her hunger. After hours of wandering, Pearl grew more than ecstatic to find a baby lobster crawling about, so she grabbed him by the carapace, pulled him from the water, and smashed his head with a rock, taking his life instantly. Unfortunately, the guilt of killing an innocent creature ate away at her, when she quickly realized she had no way of cooking it. She tried eating him raw, yet with the first bite, she threw up bile instantly. She regretted taking its life, and she wished it to be hers instead. As the sun went down and the moon came up, Pearl stayed awake through the nights, cold, fireless, and still absolutely petrified.

On the third day, she found herself wandering the jungle yet again, starving, dehydrated, and unraveling at the seams. As she searched for anything or anyone to help her, she could not bear but listen to her monkey mind chattering louder in her ears than ever before. Her thoughts grew more prominent and more demeaning, criticizing her every move and every decision. *Why would you go that way? You aren't going to find anything that way. You're so stupid. You're never going to make it, so why don't you just give up now? Why are you still trying? What are you trying to live for? You know you'd be better off dead.* As she lumbered through the jungle, the voices of her thoughts grew even louder. At first, all she heard were the voices within, whispering one thing after another after another. The thoughts became so conniving and overpowering that her head began to pound in pain. It felt as if a migraine had taken over her, and suddenly, amidst the chaos in her skull, a loud, metallic screech began to echo the entire island. The screech rang so violently that her ears felt as if they were about to bleed.

Pearl cuffed both her ears with her hands and tucked her chin into her chest, bending her torso over and crouching down into a little ball. It was as if she was slowly being taken down in the war she had with herself. As the metallic screech shrieked only louder and more ruthlessly, Pearl dropped down to her knees and let out another screech of her own, with tears dripping down her cheeks. While the horrific sound continued to echo in one ear and out the other, Pearl's vision slowly grew obscured and blurred. White stars began twinkling in her eyes and her head felt like a spinning top. With one deep gasp, Pearl collapsed forward and fainted on the spot.

4

Pearl peeled her crusted eyes open and blinked a dozen times. She lifted her head and looked around her, still trying to focus her hazy eyes.

The daylight had vanished into the night, and she could barely see a thing. Placing her palms into the dirt, she pushed herself up to a seated position, recollecting where she had been, how she got there, and exactly how long she had been laying there. *A few hours? Days? Weeks?* She wondered. One thing she did remember was the little boy with a thousand teeth chasing her through the mahogany door. *Then, I saw him on the beach!* She reminded herself. That is when reality hit her; she remained in the outer limits of The Maze within her mind.

She pushed herself up and looked down at her body. With the little light she had, she noticed dust and dirt clumped all over her arms and legs. Pearl brushed the unwanted grime off her limbs, then brushed her hands together. She squinted her eyes, looked all around, and found herself standing in a jungle, underneath a full moon. With a conscious, yet petrified deep breath in through her nose, and a deeper sigh out of her mouth, she continued on her journey.

5

Pearl walked aimlessly into the depths of the jungle. She held onto opposite arms, covering her body to keep as warm as she could. She had no idea where she was going, nor what she would do when she got there. Clueless, she walked under the moonlight that shined through the patches of leaves above her. As she made her way, she felt an overwhelming sensation of being watched, like someone was following her. She could not tell if it was just her mind psyching herself out, if someone truly was there with her, or both. Despite the unease, she continued forward into the unknown.

More time passed. Suddenly, she heard rustling in a bush beside her. Pearl jumped back, stood her ground, and prepared to fight. But, there was no need for a fight when a cute, harmless rabbit hopped out of the bush.

Pearl practically jumped out of her skin. He hopped away, leaving Pearl alone with her thoughts once again.

Pearl closed her eyes, squeezing them tight. She took a deep breath in through her nose, and a greater exhale out of her mouth. *Come on, girl, get it together. Keep your head on straight. You got this, just keep moving.* She opened her eyes, this time with determination, and continued to walk.

Time dragged like there was no tomorrow, because maybe, there wasn't one. *First, I was walking along the side of a road, then I was kidnaped, then in a forest, then in a red building, and now, I'm on a deserted island. None of this makes sense,* she thought to herself. She pondered her circumstances and questioned why this was happening to her. *Why me? Why can I never catch a break? Nobody will ever understand how I feel.* Her conniving thoughts began racing once again until suddenly, she noticed the smell of something burning. Pearl pointed her nose up to the sky and took a mighty whiff in. *Yep, something is definitely burning,* she thought.

6

She headed toward the scent, moving anxiously, yet alert. Suddenly, between the rustling leaves and wooden branches, she caught sight of flames burning from afar. For a moment, she stopped in her tracks and stared at the fire, debating whether or not to approach it. She looked left, right, and left again, held onto her breath, then tip-toed toward the fire.

She placed her hands on two giant palms, moved them out of her way, and stepped up to the flames. Still, she stood alone, not another person in sight. *How did this fire start? Someone must be here,* she thought. *I am not alone.*

Pearl looked around the fire to see if she could find anything that could clue her in. There sat a pile of wood, thrown together rather than stacked, a stick that was sharpened into a spear, and a shabby, brown sac. Pearl grabbed the sac first, rifling through to see what could be. It was empty. Next, she grabbed the spear. She rubbed her thumb against the tip; sharp was an understatement. She examined the craftsmanship of the spear, stroking its side and gripping it firmly in her hands.

"What are you doing here?" A deep, raspy voice spoke behind her.

Pearl swung her body around fast, coming face to face with a middle-aged man who wore a torn-up t-shirt and faded blue jeans. He had a scraggly, black beard and a bushy mustache that curled through his teeth. He appeared human, until he took another step closer over the fire, shining light on his crazed, black eyes. Startled, Pearl stepped back, hiding the spear behind her. Her lips quivered and she could not find the words to speak.

"Who are you?" The man asked demandingly, stepping toward Pearl with his arms out wide.

Pearl froze in terror.

"Who the fuck are you??" The man grew angrier, growing louder and more menacing. He prowled over to Pearl. Pearl stepped back in shock, until a giant tree in her path stopped her.

"I—I—"

"Are you looking through my shit?"

Pearl shook her head frantically. "No, I, I—"

"Are you alone?" The man asked.

"I—I thought I was," Pearl responded nervously. "I thought I was the only one on this whole island."

"You thought?"

"Well, yeah. There was this boy with a thousand teeth following me when I first got here. And now, you're here." Pearl explained, her hair sticking up and off her skin.

The man squinted at Pearl, then let out a loud belly laugh. He walked over to Pearl, chuckling to himself with his hands on his stomach. He put his hands on the tree behind her, locking her in place. He brought his face close to hers, squinted his eyes, then whispered into her ear. "You are never alone, here." Suddenly, the man let out a laugh that was so loud, it echoed through the jungle. The crazy look in his eyes grew even more mad as he guffawed to himself.

Instantly, Pearl's flesh flooded with fear and anxiety. Without thinking twice, she pulled the spear out from behind her back, and thrusted it into his neck, right behind his chin. His bellowed laugh morphed into silence, all while Pearl kept her grip tight and continued forcing the spear deeper inside him. Suddenly, she pulled the spear out of his neck as she tried to stab him a second time.

It was as if the wound had no effect. In an instant, the man grabbed her by the wrist and stopped her defense. Immediately, she dropped the spear, shook the man off her, and escaped his trap. She ran out from his arms and sprinted away as fast as she could.

"Come back here, baby!" The man screamed at the top of his lungs, shaking the jungle with his voice. Pearl jumped over stumps, past monstrous trees, and through walls of leaves. Sweat ran down the side of her face and every breath felt faster than the one before. She moved quickly, retreating into the darkness, until suddenly, the jungle opened to the edge of a tall cliff. Pearl came to an immediate stop. She glanced over the edge and found herself standing about five hundred feet high. "Oh, fuck," Pearl said to herself.

"Where do you think you're going?" The man spoke once again, laughing to himself. He stood outside the jungle, lurking closer toward Pearl with blood seeping from his neck. He looked mad, not just angry, but simply out of his mind. He brought his hands out wide, holding the bloody spear Pearl had stabbed him with.

Pearl stepped back onto the edge of the cliff. A few rocks underneath her feet tumbled from the mountain and rolled down its side. Pearl looked down, then back up at the man. Underneath the moonlight, the two of them stood, prey versus predator. The man stepped closer, so close he could grab Pearl if he tried, but instinctively, with a single breath and a thought that said, "this is it" Pearl took one more step back. She stepped off the earth, and gravity did the rest. Immediately, her vision went black.

# Door #2
# I Am Trapped

1

Pearl's eyes opened abrupt and wide. She gasped, and her entire body convulsed like she had been shocked back to life. That first breath felt like the first one she had ever taken in her entire life. Her back shot up and off the floor, her sit bones kept grounded into the floor, and her spine sat up tall. At the top of her breath in, she flung her hands onto her chest and hugged her torso. Finally, her exhausted exhalation poured out of her mouth, as she felt her arms, her legs, and every other inch of her body. Her following breaths dragged heavily, and she sounded as if she had just ran ten miles in ten minutes.

Pearl sat up hopeless, for a moment, as she recollected her mind and breath. She began to look around her, her arms swinging by her sides and the hair on her skin raised tall.

All around her, tall, blood-red walls rose so high that she could not see the ceiling above. She found herself sitting in a narrow hallway, with nothing but a few, flickering lightbulbs hanging overhead. Suddenly, it hit her like a freight train. Pearl found herself back inside The Maze, except, this time, this red hallway appeared to lead to somewhere different than the one she had walked through before. It stretched out long before her, welcoming her into the unknown.

Pearl stayed rooted down into the ground while her shoulders began to melt forward in front of her body. She shoved her face into her hands and let out a hysterical cry, seeping an immeasurable number of tears. As she sobbed, the sound of chain links chiming together grabbed her attention. Pearl slowly peeled her face away from her hands and looked down at her right wrist. She counted the chain links, this time counting only nine, and the single, pink pearl. Her tears stopped for a moment, and her face transformed into an expression of confused wonder. *Weren't there ten before?* She thought to herself. Pearl examined the bracelet even more closely, wondering how she could be missing a link. She saw no tear in the string, in fact it was tied tight and secure like she had remembered.

She wondered if one had fallen off her wrist, but couldn't imagine how. Pearl quickly looked over both of her shoulders, searching for the lost chain link. She raised an eyebrow, wondering how only one was missing, yet the other nine were secure with the pearl. Alas, the only chain links she could find were the nine hanging from her wrist. Confused and uneasy, and without thinking about it much further, Pearl placed the palms of her hands into the ground and slowly pushed herself up and off of the floor. She stood slouched and held onto opposite arms, her lips quickly quivering and her breath short. Pearl's eyes filled with tears once again, yet she held onto them tight, not letting one fall. She stood in disbelief as to how she was still alive after all that she had just gone through. She had not sustained even a single scratch. *Did I just fall off a cliff? Was I dreaming? Did that really happen to me? It felt so real,* she thought. Suddenly, in that very moment, Pearl had experienced her first ego death of The Maze.

In a flash, Pearl felt an overwhelming sensation of comfort and empathy flood throughout her body. Since her life turned upside down, Pearl felt alone, and she had convinced herself that she was the only person that felt pain as painful as hers, the only one who felt sadness as sad as hers, and the only one who could suffer in life like she did. It was as if she were the only person on the planet to have gone through what she has gone through. She convinced herself that nobody in the world would ever understand how she felt; not even come close to compre-hending her pain. She had been through so much at such a young age, and she always pondered why. Yet, as she stood in The Maze, she considered her experience in the first door. Despite its horrific nature, through the darkness, it emanated light, revealing to her a valuable lesson. For the first time in her life, Pearl no longer felt alone. Unclear as to why, Pearl sensed her loneliness transform into a simple thought that consumed not only her mind, but the minds of millions. It was not her experiences in life that had made her feel alone, it was the self-limiting belief she had been telling herself all along. She realized that the pain she felt inside did not discredit the pain millions of others experienced in their lives, too. Pearl's heart was not the only one that ached in anguish. Not everyone needed to go through what Pearl had gone through in order to feel the same pain. As the feeling of loneliness dispersed from her mind and body, she still found herself caught up in her shadows. Though this realization swept over her, her truth, still, was buried deep within. It would take much more than a simple recognition of one false story to fully unleash her light. Yet, with this new realization, she felt lighter, a sensation of acceptance, and value. Pearl had shed her first layer of the onion of life. *I am not alone. I am never alone.* She thought to herself.

2

This lightness that had come over her felt uncomfortable, yet secure. She did not understand what to think about it, so she did not think much of it at all. She simply acknowledged the feeling that swept over her, and then let it go. Finding her way out of The Maze seemed to be the only thing on her mind. Although she had learned her first lesson of The Maze, she was still petrified. Pearl shifted her gaze down the hallway, swallowed dry, and began wandering forward.

Pearl skulked ahead, hugging her shoulders close to her ears while maintaining short, quiet breaths. She made her way deeper into The Maze, blindly following the hallway wherever it would take her. She wandered for what felt like forever, following the path, turning corners, and finding nothing more than tall, blood-red walls. She kept onward.

Suddenly, as she made her way deeper through The Maze, the sound of footsteps sprinting toward her from behind echoed through the hall, stomping so loudly that Pearl jumped to the side to move out of the way. Yet, when she turned her head to look back at who was running at her, she felt shocked to see that she stood alone. Her skin crawled.

"Who's there?" Pearl asked aloud.

No response back. Silence swept through the hall.

Pearl stood hesitant, debating on what to do next. She looked over her shoulder, back ahead, back over her shoulder, then forward again. This place felt too real, and she wanted nothing more than to be out of it.

She continued moving forward, slowly, and steadily. She walked for a couple more minutes down the dimly lit hall, until the sound of footsteps ran at her from behind once again. Pearl spun around. Still, she found herself alone, hysterical, and full of fear. She remained quiet this time, squinting her eyes down the red hallway. *It's too quiet,* Pearl thought to herself.

Suddenly, the hair-raising laughter of a small child echoed the hallway. It laughed mischievously, at her, not with her. The laughter sounded so eerie that it made every inch of Pearl's skin crawl. Without hesitation, Pearl turned around and sprinted down the hall.

Pearl ran until the sound of footsteps and laughter subsided. Then, silence swept the hall once again. Pearl stopped, placing her hands onto her knees to catch her breath for a moment. Her body felt fatigued, yet her mind continued to run wild. She could not grasp any of her thoughts, let alone her own breath. She let go of her knees, shifted her gaze back up, and found herself at the end of the hall. At the dead-end stood an old, tattered, wooden door, chipped and cracked throughout, with a round, shiny handle. Pearl stared at the door while her insides churned. The thought of entering another vile door made her sick to her stomach.

Then, the child's laughter began once again, growing louder and louder as if they were following her. Pearl turned around, searching for the voice in distress, yet, there was no one and nothing in sight except for the hanging lightbulbs that hovered overhead. Despite her anxiety, she knew staying here, lost in The Maze, would be way worse than seeing where this door could take her. As terror crept over her skin and through her tendons, she turned back toward the door, reached her hand forward, and gripped the knob. With a single, painful swallow and her heart beating out of her chest, she turned the knob and opened the door. In that moment, four sickly, bruised arms reached out from the other side. These lifeless looking hands grabbed ahold of Pearl's body, gripping the cotton fabric on her back between each of their skeletal fingers, and forcibly pulled her inside with them. The door slammed shut behind her on its own, and then disappeared into thin air. Pearl had entered the second door of The Maze.

3

Pearl's shriek echoed the walls of the lightless room she had been dragged into. She screamed at the top of her lungs, jolting her body back and forth with hopes to escape the chilling seize. One of the four hands quickly grabbed hold of Pearl's mouth, wrapping its cold, bony fingers around her lips, silencing her cries. Meanwhile, the other three hands pinned Pearl's arms behind her back, restricting not only her voice, but her movements, too.

The two creatures ushered Pearl deeper into the unknown. There was not one light in sight, here, and Pearl found herself blinded from where she was going, and who was manhandling her to get there. Her eyes shifted right and left and right again, as beads of sweat slowly rolled down her face.

Suddenly, as the three pairs of feet moved further into the dark, a tiny ball of light began to catch Pearl's eye from afar. This light weakly illuminated the space around it, revealing colorless walls leading into another narrow hallway. Pearl's eyes focused on the single light, as she squinted her eyes tinier and breathed in the chilled hand that hugged her lips. The constraining hands continued to push Pearl forward, closer toward the light.

One foot after another, they hastily moved. The further they walked, the brighter the light became. Suddenly, everything started to become clearer as Pearl's eyes slowly adjusted to the darkness. As they traveled closer to wherever they were taking her, the sound of soft screams shrieking, and shackles rattling sounded through the hall before her. As they walked further, the screams grew louder, like drums pounding in her ears.

The end of the hallway slowly became more visible. At the end of the tunnel, she noticed a dirt wall reflecting the flickering light hanging from above, swaying by the skin of one's teeth. As the three of them lurched closer, she noticed the tunnel turn to the left, guiding her deeper into the unknown.

With a peek of light, Pearl shifted her head over her left and right shoulder, as she examined who or what it was that was forcing her down the tunnel and toward what she believed to be the last moments of her life. Her sight revealed a scene no less than horrific.

Holding Pearl hostage in their arms were two tall creatures with bodies made of nothing more than skin and bones. Blood seeped from their insides out, pouring from their patches of missing skin that exposed their bones and flesh, yet the skin still growing over them appeared grey, cold, and dead. When she gazed up at their faces, their sunken-in eyes glared back down at her, piercing through her soul like a jab of a knife. They had extremely small and pointed noses, and they both had three mouths lined up, side by side, each one drooling with wicked smiles and heavy jaws.

Pearl's head shook back and forth, while her pupils swallowed her irises. Her heart pounded practically out of her chest and her screams of terror grew louder.

In an instant, she pulled her arms back to her body as she glued her feet down into the floor beneath her. She jolted her arms and elbows with severe force, intending to escape the arms of the two creatures. The cold hand covering her mouth gripped deeper onto Pearl's lips. It squeezed her cheeks and pulled her head closer toward its dismantled body, concealing her voice, her strength, and her will to fight.

Fear lingered throughout Pearl's whole body. Pearl's chest puffed up and down and she huffed in and out of her nose. Suddenly, one of the creature's skeletal hands wrapped around her lower back and pushed her forward, forcing her to continue ahead.

The three of them approached the back dirt wall and stood beside the dangling, flickering light. They followed the hallway and turned the corner, traveling past the light, as they continued their way deeper down the walkway. Eventually, more hanging bulbs began to appear the further they traveled, bringing more light to Pearl's new surroundings. She found herself traveling down what looked like an underground tunnel. Dirt, pebbles, and rocks surrounded her, comprising the walls and ceiling above them. The further they traveled toward the unidentified destination, the narrower the dirt tunnel became, eventually leading to what appeared to be another passage at the end of the hall, lit and full of ruckus. With every step they took, the mysterious, helpless cries grew into terrorized screams. As the three of them made their way closer, Pearl's stomach crawled up into her throat and she could barely catch a single breath.

Pearl walked below the hanging lights, restrained between the two creatures, heading closer toward the petrified screams. Her feet shuffled and dragged across the dirt, walking down the long, narrow hall. Tears rolled down from her tortured eyes and despite all that she had been through during her time in The Maze so far, she was mortal, and fear was her master. She gulped and broke another sweat.

Finally, they made it to their destination. They made their way into the wave of vibration, a wave of voices that spoke and screamed loudly, ferociously, and full of woe. The passage led them into an area full of horrendous looking, barred prison cells. The cells were tightly compact and side by side. They looked to be centuries old and like they had never been cleaned before. The floor was covered with dirt, sand, grime, and feces from both mortals and immortals, and the air felt so thick she could practically choke on it. It reeked of rot and death, and the smell became so unbearable that Pearl began to dry heave in the devilish hand that covered her quivering lips.

They continued going further down into the tunnel, passing cell, after cell, after cell. Each unit had at least one prisoner held captive. As she walked ahead, she examined everyone in sight. For a moment, she believed her eyes to be deceiving her. She really was in a nightmare and could not wake up.

The prisoners appeared all uniquely, yet unimaginably different. Some appeared human, while others did not. Some of them looked hopeless, while others appeared wicked and not of this world—whatever *this* world was. The ones that looked to be human sat along the back walls of the cell like children in a time-out. They sat weak, defeated, and in despair, with their heads falling heavily between their knees. She noticed them with wonder, yet, the immortals grabbed Pearl's attention even more.

The disturbed, otherworldly creatures stood tall against the cell doors. She noticed a few with pure white eyes, others with razor sharp teeth and some; with no teeth at all. One of them even had his lips sewn shut with a simple thread and needle. She noticed some of them speckled with warts like slimy, green toads, some with scales like a reptilian, and others with skin that chipped like a decaying zombie. Some prowled on two legs, while others scavenged on all fours. Many of the creatures stood hunched over beside the cell with their hands wrapped around the metal bars, shaking and banging them with their fists. Some were howling, some were laughing, some were catcalling, and others were hooting. Human or not, one thing they all had in common was not only were they all trapped in The Maze, but they were all extremely interested in the new meat coming through. The underground tunnel echoed of voices that spoke over one another.

"Look, it's a seeker!"

"New blood!"

"She's a seeker!"

"What's your name, baby?"

"Want to come in here with me?"

"New flesh!"

"We got a seeker, everybody!"

"Make yourself at home!" The voices screamed.

Pearl immediately felt her heart drop down into the pit of her stomach. *What is a seeker? What are they talking about? Where the fuck am I? What is happening??* Pearl thought intensely to herself, tightening every muscle in her body as she forcibly continued forward.

Finally, the creatures directed her toward one of the gut-wrenching cells. One of the creatures released their grip from Pearl to unlock the door, while the other creature held onto her tightly. He jammed the key into the lock, fumbled through the tumblers, and unlocked the door. He pulled the cage door open, while the other three-mouthed monster led her inside.

Pearl rooted her heels into the ground and put on a fight to get in. Her body jolted left and right, and she even tried to escape the grip of the creature that held on. Finally, after a few moments of struggle, the other creature grabbed a hold of Pearl, and the two of them together had more than enough strength to throw her in. With no remorse, they tossed Pearl like dirty clothes into a laundry basket. She tripped on her own feet and tumbled down into the ground face first. She laid there, limp, weak, and worn to the bone, as the two monstrous creatures slammed her cell closed behind her. One of them stood behind while the other locked the chamber. He pulled his keys out from the lock, and slowly redirected his vision toward Pearl. With a shady, small smile slithering across his face, he grinned at her, piercing his eyes through her like a knife. Then, both creatures made their way back to wherever it was they had come from.

4

Limp and worn out, Pearl laid face down into the dirt. Snot dripped out of her nose and drool hung from her bottom lip. Her quivering lips trembled on their own, and a single tear seeped from her right eye and trickled down her cheek. She crawled her hands underneath her wobbly elbows and pushed herself up, peeling herself off the dirt floor. As she slowly lifted her head, she noticed a sad soul sitting miserably in the cell with her.

This person sat quietly in a tiny ball, hugging their knees into their chest, and hiding their face. The person sat so still that one would think they were lifeless if it were not for the tight grip they had around their own body. However, this person had skin like hers, hair on their head, and normal clothes on their back. He appeared to be a mortal like Pearl, trapped within The Maze of his mind, too. Pearl was reluctantly interested.

She pushed herself up to a seated position, slowly maneuvering her way toward the dirt wall. She pressed her back into the dirt behind her and brought her knees close to her chest, too. She stuttered with hesitation.

"He—hello?"

The individual made no movements. It was as if this person had seen and done it all, like curiosity had killed more than the cat. In fact, curiosity might as well have brutally murdered any last bits of interest this individual may have had. Pearl raised an eyebrow high.

"Excuse me?" She spoke again, in hopes of a response. Again, the person remained tucked into their body, silent and still.

Pearl slowly peeled her back off the dirt wall and hovered over to the prisoner. She crawled over on her hands and knees, staying quiet with every move she made. Lifting her right hand, she lightly tapped them on their knee. In an instant, the man jumped and squealed like a dying pig, as if he had just awoken from a nightmare. His scrawny, shaky arms jolted up and crossed over his face like an X, shielding himself away from Pearl.

"Please spare me! Don't hurt me anymore, please!"

"I'm sorry! I didn't mean to startle you," Pearl admitted, jolting back herself.

"Who are you!? What do you want!?" The man asked frantically, looking back at Pearl. His eyes appeared human, blood shot from tears endlessly flooding his vision, and his chapped lips quivered as if he had been tortured for years.

"I'm Pearl. I was just brought here. I noticed you are like me; a human..." Pearl spoke nervously with a soft voice.

The man fell quiet.

"Were you brought here, too? Into The Maze?" She continued.

The man recollected his staggered breath and rested his hunched back against the dirt wall behind him. He glared at Pearl dead in the eyes, and responded, "I have been here forever. I can't even remember what it is like to be anywhere other than this fucking place."

"You never found your way out?" Pearl asked him.

"It is not that I never found my way out of The Maze. I simply was not strong enough to make it out. I belong in this cell. I belong in this mental hell." The man rested his head back onto his knees, hugging them tightly against his chest.

"Why do you think that?"

The man peeked out from his crossed arms. "Because why else would I still be here?"

"Well, that's what I am wondering, too."

The man rolled his eyes. He lifted his right hand and pointed at his wrist. "See this?"

Pearl did not understand. She raised another eyebrow. "Your wrist?"

The man grew irritated. He reached for Pearl's wrist and pointed at her chain-linked bracelet.

"My bracelet?"

"Yes. You still have yours. I don't." He lifted his chin and rested the back of his head against the wall.

"You had the same bracelet as me? Did Doc give it to you, too?"

The man closed his eyes as he spoke, like he could not bear to even speak the words coming from his mouth. "Not the exact same one. They are all different. They all have one pearl, but they all have a different amount of chain links attached. Just depends on how many lessons the person needs to learn." He refrained from answering the second question.

"What are you talking about?" Pearl asked, confused yet interested. *Lessons? What lessons?*

"You're in for a rude awakening." The man rested his head back down on his knees, shielding his face from Pearl.

Pearl's eyebrows furrowed toward one another. She did not understand why the man was being so rude to her, or why he would not help her. *Wouldn't he want to escape with her? Why did he stop trying?* Pearl pondered.

"Can you just—"

"LEAVE ME BE!" The man demanded, shooting a scowl at her. He quickly grew short and uninterested in Pearl, and it became clear that he wanted nothing more to do with her. Pearl flinched at the tone of his voice, sat back onto the floor, and crawled over to the other side of the cell by herself.

5

As hours passed by, Pearl eventually fell asleep. She lay on the floor with her head rested on one bicep in the fetal position, curling up into a ball to stay warm. All the cells had grown quiet over time once the new blood had settled amongst them. Just about everyone and everything had fallen asleep or kept to themselves, leaving nothing but silence to sweep the cells.

Suddenly, the entire prison began to shake. Everyone and everything trapped behind bars was awoken to the vibration of stampeding feet coming from the other side of the tunnel. The cells grew lively once again. Pearl pushed herself up to a seated position and sat back against the dirt wall. Some of the prisoners jumped up and over to their cell doors, some crawled over, while others remained seated. The man sharing the cell with Pearl lifted his head from his knees. He looked out toward the tunnel, glanced over toward her, then back toward the tunnel.

"What's going on?" Pearl asked him.

The man shot another glance at Pearl. While his lips stayed shut, he wore an expression on his face that said, "something bad is about to happen".

Pearl's eyes grew wide as she received his unspoken words. She stared down the tunnel along with the rest of the prisoners.

The stampeding footsteps grew louder. Suddenly, the same two creatures that had dragged her in before ran out from around the corner. Behind them emerged a tall, thin man cloaked in black from head to toe, hiding half of his face underneath a draped, black hood.

"Where is the seeker?" The covered man asked in a low voice.

Instantaneously, adrenaline pumped through Pearl's veins and her heart beat out of her chest. The eyes of every prisoner glanced over at Pearl, while she sat like a deer in headlights, pressing her back even further into the wall behind her.

The man in all black walked between the creatures, making his way further down the tunnel, passing cell after cell, until he came face to face with Pearl's cell. First, he looked at the man sitting across from Pearl, then glanced toward Pearl. "You are the seeker?" He asked her.

Pearl's eyes grew wider and began to tear up. "I—I don't know what you're talking about."

The man chuckled to himself. He looked over his shoulder toward one of three-mouthed creatures. "Give me the keys."

One of the monsters handed him a metal ring with an excessive number of keys hanging from it. He looked through the bunch, picked out one, rusted key, and slid it into the lock, opening her cell door wide.

"Take him out of here," the man ordered the minions, pointing at Pearl's cellmate. The creatures scurried inside, picked up her cellmate, tied his arms behind his back, and walked him out of the cell. He walked out leisurely and without a fight, as if he had done this a thousand times already. His willingness to comply scared Pearl even more.

The man cloaked in black walked into the cell. Pearl continued to sit with her back against the wall, petrified and uneasy. She stared up at the man like a lost puppy. All eyes were locked on Pearl.

"Welcome to The Maze, Pearl. You should be honored to be here. Isn't this place magical?" He looked down at her with an eerie smile, exposing only about six rotting teeth barely hanging from his diseased gums.

Pearl remained silent, as she looked at him like he was the devil himself.

"Can I have your bracelet?" He asked her, keeping his grin. He stuck his hand out with his palm facing up.

Pearl glanced down at her wrist and the chain links hanging on. She covered it with her other hand and looked around toward the others who were held captive in their cells. Those who appeared human had nothing but naked wrists. She thought about what her cellmate said, about how he no longer carried his. As if he had, but something had happened to it. Then she remembered what Doc had told her before she was put into this place; about how vital this hideous piece of jewelry was for her journey. Something inside her did not feel right. Pearl glared back up toward the man.

"Why?" She asked.

The man laughed out loud, sticking his hand out even more. "I suppose you misunderstood my question. Give me your bracelet."

Pearl swallowed. She looked around at the prisoners once again and noticed them all staring back at her silently and wide-eyed, as if they were watching a car wreck. *Why would this bracelet be so vital in a place like this? What significance does this bracelet have on these people? Did it have value? Or was it equivalent to life or death?* Pearl thought to herself. She looked back at the man and his empty hand.

"No."

Every prisoner's jaw dropped to the floor. The room echoed with gasps, as they continued to watch the scene unfold. The man's smile quickly faded, and he lowered his hand back down by his side, taken back. "Did—did you just say no?"

"I'm not giving you my bracelet," she asserted. "It's the last thing I'll do."

The man's face grew furious and tenser than ever. "Give me your bracelet, now," he demanded.

"No," Pearl argued back.

The man balled his hand into a fist and shook with rage. He then released his shaking fist, brought both hands up to his hood, and pulled back the cloak from over the top of his head, exposing himself fully for the first time. The top of his head appeared hairless with lesions all over his skull. His eyes uncovered a sight of pure malevolence. His pupils were red, and they stretched tall and skinny, like a cat's. He stared down at Pearl with anger burning in his eyes.

Pearl shifted her weight forward and placed her hands into the ground. Before she had the chance to push herself up to her feet, the man became engulfed with rage. He picked up his right foot, then slammed it down with all his might on top of Pearl's right hand, followed by her left, leaving her with nothing but broken bones underneath her bruised skin. She screamed at the top of her lungs as the man reached down, picked her up by her shirt, and pressed her back into the wall. Her feet hovered over the dirt, and she cried helplessly.

"Give me your bracelet!" He shouted.

"Go fuck yourself," she hissed back at him, with tears rolling down her face.

"You think you are the master of your own mind? Well guess what?" The man touched his nose to Pearl's nose and breathed into her mouth.

His voice lowered even more. "Get ready to spend the rest of eternity in hell with us, you fucking coward. Trapped; like the rest of us." The man pulled her away from the wall, for a moment, and then slammed her back against it.

Pearl cleared her throat and spit on his face. The man dropped Pearl to the ground, leaving her helpless and incapable of fighting. He wiped her saliva out of his eye, shook it off his hand, and made his way back to the cell door, locking her inside, alone. "The Maze will claim her in the next door," he mentioned to the rest of the prisoners and his scrawny minions. "She wants to learn the hard way. So be it. Give me the lever."

One of the monsters ran down the path they came from. A few moments later, he trotted back with a grey, metal box with a small knob that had several gauges on top, and a small lever underneath. The prisoners went wild and cheered with rapture.

The man turned the knob to one of the gauges, then grabbed the lever. Before making any sudden movements, the man scowled at Pearl and left her with a few last words. "We will see you soon." With little effort, the man pulled the lever down. Like an earthquake, her cell, and her cell only, began to tremble. Dirt fell from the walls, the ceilings, and began crumbling all around her. Suddenly, from the center of the cell, the floor began to open, revealing a giant hole beneath that stretched into a black abyss, gaping so deep that she could not see the bottom. The dirt below Pearl began rolling toward the yawning pit. She jumped onto her feet, hugged the dirt wall, and huffed and puffed for breath. The prisoners continued to watch her fight for her life, shouting and cheering with excitement. The ground crumbled even further and quickly grew steeper. She stood on her toes against the wall, when suddenly, she ran out of room. In the midst of the cheers and applause from prisoners, and with a single screech, gravity took Pearl down, and she fell into the abyss. Everything went black.

# DOOR #3
# I CANNOT BREATHE

1

Pearl's back shot up and off the floor, as though she had been shocked back to life. She looked around herself for a moment, examining her new surroundings. She found herself looking at tall, painted red walls with cracks splitting throughout, a few lightbulbs swaying back and forth up above, and another long, narrow hallway stretching out in front of her. Alas, she had returned to The Maze.

Her breath raced in and out as she sat, nearly defeated. She shoved her face into the palms of her hands and let out another desperate cry. Yet, as she blubbered like a baby, each tear that fell from her face felt revitalizing. She sat with her emotions, allowing herself to feel all of the pain that surfaced within her. In that moment, Pearl paused. She slowly lifted her face from her hands, stared off into space, and uncovered her second lesson of The Maze.

As Pearl sat back in The Maze, exhausted, fearful, and practically out of breath, she realized that she had a choice to be a prisoner of her own mind, or be free from her chains. It became clear to her that the time she spent feeling trapped was not a negative place to be in, rather, it was a wake-up call. This overwhelming realization of her own liberty shifted her perspective enough to see it as not a feeling, but rather, a message. What was her body trying to really tell her when she felt this sensation? Did she feel trapped? Or did she just simply believe she was? The truth is, she had never been trapped; in fact, this idea of being trapped was nothing more than another story she had been telling herself all along. Although this was only the second shadow she had shined her flashlight on so far, she had plenty more to uncover. She noticed her attachment to her limiting thought, yet she still did not fully understand. This was simply a taste of what was to come. Still, she felt exceedingly prideful for staying strong through the last door of The Maze, standing up for herself all the while shedding another layer. She stood up for her ground and refused to give her bracelet away, which got her thinking elsewhere.

Pearl blinked the glaze over her eyes away, returned to center, and shot a glance at her wrist. She felt immediately relieved to find the bracelet still hanging from her wrist. She thought to herself, *why did he want this so bad? What was so special about this piece of string?* As she mused, she began to count the chain links hanging from the string.

*One, two, three, four, five, six, seven, eight,* she counted in her head. *Eight links? Didn't I have nine last time? How did I lose another?* Pearl wondered to herself, puzzled with disbelief. She looked over her shoulders and on the floor by her sides, yet nothing was there. She counted the links one more time, just to be sure. "One, two, three, four, five, six, seven... eight." She counted right the first time. Her eyebrows drew together, then she pierced down the long, narrow hall. Pushing herself up from the ice-cold ground, she rolled her shoulders back down her spine, and filled her lungs with air like a balloon. On her exhale, she let out a long, rejuvenating sigh, letting go of the weight of the lesson she had learned. She began down her path in The Maze, once again.

2

Pearl walked alertly and stealthily. Up ahead, she noticed the hall turn left, welcoming her further down a path of uncharted territory. She swallowed a dry lump down her throat and tiptoed her way further.

As she finally reached the end of this hallway, she hesitantly peeked her head around the corner to examine the new, upcoming space. This next hallway stretched unusually long out in front of her. It stretched about fifty feet long and stopped with a blood-red dead end. However, in this hall, Pearl noticed that along these walls, there stood about five different doors on both walls, totaling ten doors in this path. Each door appeared to be the same, all made of old, tattered wood and each had its own beautiful, bronze doorknob.

Confused she felt and clueless as to how she had gotten there once again, Pearl felt unfamiliar, uncomfortable, and uncertain. Immediately, she realized that the only way for her to escape would be to open another door. Her stomach fell.

She walked ahead as she examined the doors around her. She faced each one, trying to determine whether any had differences to compare. Yet, they all stood identical. *Which one do I choose?* With ten options in front of her, she grew stumped.

Pearl grazed her hands along the walls, rubbing her fingers against each door. She made her way to the end of the hall, facing the blank red wall at the end. Pearl spun her body back around, gazed down the hall, and evaluated which door to choose once again.

She felt too overwhelmed with options. Suddenly, she reached her right hand toward the door closest to her at the end of the hall and gripped the bronze knob between her fingers, pulling it open. It swung out wide, welcoming Pearl to the next chapter. Pearl could not believe her eyes.

On the other side of the door stood a massive, moving wall of water. Through the wall of water, she witnessed various types of fish swimming peacefully on the other side. The floor was covered with trillions of grains of sand, and she noticed patches of seaweed that grew hundreds of feet tall, swaying slowly back and forth. Rays of sunlight that shined from above illuminated the water and brought light to her surroundings. Pearl stood face to face with the bottom of the ocean.

She reached her hand out in front of her to touch the wall of water. With her index finger, she poked the water, slowly sliding her finger through the other side, until her hand was fully submerged in water. The water felt cold. She pulled her hand back and opened her palm out wide. She gazed down at her hand and watched the water trickle off her fingertips, while dripping down her forearm.

"Hell no, I am not going in there." Pearl grabbed the door and slammed it shut.

She turned her body around to walk away from the door. Yet, in the blink of an eye, her whole body suddenly became submerged underwater. The tattered, wooden door before her had disappeared into thin air, leaving her standing alone at the bottom of the ocean with nothing but the clothes on her back and the bracelet around her wrist.

3

Fear swept over her, and Pearl gasped for a breath. Her entire body jolted from being in a daze, and she simply could not fathom what her eyes were seeing. However, as she gasped air, not water, entered her body and filled her lungs up with space. She held her breath for a moment, her mind frazzled and confused, yet she noticed a lack of pressure on her head, and she felt no different than she did on land. She swayed her right hand back and forth to feel the water around her. She observed the ripples of the water rushing through her fingers, yet her hands remained dry. She could feel the texture of the water, yet it did not seem to affect her skin. Her hair kept dry and continued to rest lightly on her shoulders. Even her vision remained clear. Her eyesight did not blur, nor did her eyes feel pain from being open underwater. Pearl blinked to make sure her eyes were not playing tricks. It was as if she stood inside a bubble of air, yet, she could feel the water wash all around her. Uneasy, she released her exhale, deflating her lungs as her breath poured from her lips. In this door, a breath never felt so pure. In this door, she could breathe underwater. In this door, she felt like she could simply breathe.

"What the fuck is this," Pearl spoke aloud, stating rather than asking. She shifted her gaze all around her, noticing fish of all kinds, seaweed dancing through the subtle flow of the current, and the contrasting mixtures of sand lying below her feet. She saw beautiful, vibrant coral reefs growing wild and free, and she noticed red, orange, and purple starfish sprawled out long over ocean rocks. Sponges lived in every different direction, sea urchins sat with caution, and crabs both big and small scrambled all over the sand. Pearl perceived the remarkable life under sea, above and below her, that lived on for miles. Despite the fresh air flowing through her lungs, Mother Nature's beauty took her breath away.

Pearl took her first step forward, followed by her second. Soon after, she noticed herself wandering underwater, still breathing fresh oxygen in and out of her body. She roamed the seafloor, weightless. At first, she moved slowly with stealth, but as time passed by, nature's artistry captured her attention even more. For the first time in The Maze, she felt a sensation of calmness come over her as she grew mesmerized by the outstanding beauty before her.

She absorbed the unfamiliar territory like she had been missing it for years. She felt so at peace watching every living creature simply just *be*. Overhead, she witnessed stingrays fluttering freely, giant sea turtles casually passing by, and sea lions causing havoc with one another like a pack of puppies. She even witnessed a pod of dolphins drift by, playing with one another without a worry in the world. She laughed, looking with bright eyes up at all the life before her. Pearl watched these forms of life like she was watching her inner child, playing freely in the present moment. In that moment, her heart beat slowed and she became at ease as anxiety and fear dispersed from her pores.

She swanned along the seafloor, her arms slowly swaying by her sides. Her eyes looked every which way, observing the Earth's creations. Amongst the captivation, she forgot she had ever entered The Maze. She was absorbed in an abundance of tranquility, peace, and happiness, and it was as if the world had frozen around her, and all she had was time.

4

Time passed as Pearl wandered ahead. As she ambled forward, the water around her began to grow more cold and crisp. Instantly, a feeling of distress sparked through her whole body. Her feet came to a stop and sunk a couple inches into the sand below her. Pearl looked around her and noticed the sea creatures briskly disperse the area. Within no more than one minute, Pearl stood at the bottom of the ocean, alone.

Pearl looked in every direction around her. Wondering where the life before her had gone, her skin began speckling like a goose, and the hair on her arms rose tall. She shifted her gaze down at her arms and then crossed them into her chest. Her shoulders rose taller toward her ears and her breath began to grow short.

Suddenly, the rays of sunlight that shined through the water began fading before her, leaving behind nothing but darkness. Before Pearl knew it, the ocean grew black, and she stood in silence. Pearl spun her body around, frantically looking in all different directions. She could see nothing, but she still felt the sand under foot and the subtle movement of the water all around. *What the fuck is going on?* She wondered.

Gradually, a pressure in her head started to form. Her head began to ache and her ears started to pop. The ocean temperature continued to rapidly decrease, growing colder and more frigid than ever before. The familiar feeling of terror began creeping through her veins once again.

Out of nowhere, she felt a gush of water hit her back, so much so that it pushed her forward. She spun around and squinted to see the cause, but everywhere she looked appeared to be the same; black. Pearl's sense of direction had faded with the light, as she could only see three feet in front of her. She had gone from standing in a clear, blue ocean with life all around, to submerged in the pit of the deepest, darkest trench in the ocean. Her stomach began to churn. She took a short breath in, and a shorter breath out.

While Pearl stood in fear, a weary awareness grew within. Her eyes focused on her view a few feet ahead, for that was all that she could make out. As soon as Pearl's eyes focused, she witnessed a grey fin three times the size of her head swim past her. She immediately covered her mouth with her hands, and her whole body froze with anticipation. Pearl knew that it was at this moment that her hunter had found its prey.

The creature came into sight again. This time, its whole body swam slowly in front of Pearl. She noticed its rough, grey body that had dark stripes vertically along its sides, as she watched it slowly fade back into the dark. She stood solid, yet her insides felt like they were melting. Another minute passed by, and the animal made its way back in front of her, swimming closer toward the ocean floor. The beast swam closer to her, this time making direct eye contact with Pearl. Pearl was, in fact, faced with what could have been the biggest Tiger Shark that she could have ever imagined.

*This is it. This is the end,* Pearl thought to herself. Stunned, she squeezed her eyes shut and held onto her arms. Suddenly, the hair on Pearl's head began to slowly lift up and off of her shoulders, rising above her skull, flowing through the water back and forth. It was as if gravity had finally caught up with her in the ocean depths.

On Pearl's next breath in, a trickle of water passed through her lips and dripped down into her lungs. She coughed lightly, clearing her throat on her next exhale. On her next inhale, more water traveled through her mouth, swimming its way into her lungs. Unfortunately, this breath invited much more liquid into her space, which caused Pearl to cough ferociously. She began to choke, and she could not stop gagging on the water. She gasped for another breath in, dropping down onto her knees and placing her hands onto the sand. In the midst of choking for her last bit of air, the

Tiger Shark swam out before her once again. As it passed, swimming away into oblivion, hiding behind the murky water appeared the little boy with a thousand teeth. A smile crept across his face and he began laughing hysterically at Pearl. Petrified, Pearl gasped for her third and final breath, when instantly, her lungs completely filled with water. She dropped down to her forearms while her whole body contracted in misery. She plopped down onto her side, rolling over to her back. Her vision began to pixelate, everything turning blacker than it already was. Just like that, she could no longer breathe. She opened her mouth wide from exhaustion, as she could not bear the sensation of water traveling through her airways any longer. Bubbles gushed out from her mouth and floated up to the surface. Pearl gazed up as she watched them float away. In those last few seconds, she felt her lungs combust and explode inside of her. The little boy looked down on her, giggling to himself at Pearl's despair. Her vision went black.

# Door #4
## The World is Swallowing Me

## 1

*Gasp.*

A gush of breath shot through Pearl's lungs, shocking her system with life once again. Her back shot up and off the red, cold floor of The Maze, as she gulped for a deep breath in. Water dripped from her lips and her eyes stung. She began wiping the water off of her, shaking the bracelet on her wrist side to side. The sound of the chain links clanging one another caught Pearl's attention. However, the bracelet looked different than the time before. Pearl counted each link one by one, for a total of seven, one less than the last time she counted. *Seven? Weren't there eight links last time? How do I keep losing them?* Pearl thought to herself with confusion. Suddenly, amid her wonder, she took a conscious inhalation while her mind went adrift.

With that inhalation, Pearl felt her breath flow calmly and easily; unlike ever before. She tuned into her breath, as she watched it flow in and out her lungs. She had never seen anything like it before. Up until she had entered the third door of The Maze, her life force that flowed throughout her body constantly felt constricted and burnt-out. She lived swamped with uncertainty, leaving her short of breaths for so many years of her young life. She believed she could never catch a break, let alone a simple breath. Yet, as she sat, just about defeated in The Maze once again, and with this new awareness of breath, every breath there on out flowed replenished, refreshed, and revitalized. Even the rhythm of her heartbeat pumped easily and without effort. Pearl felt as if a hulking weight had been taken off her chest, and she had been given permission to finally breathe freely. She no longer felt as if she were suffocating on the chaos life brought her way, and she became aware that she had the power to make her involuntary breath voluntary. She no longer allowed herself to get caught up with unmanageable breaths. Rather, she had learned it was her, and only her, who controlled the life force that flowed throughout her being. With the power of breath, she released a cleansing sigh of relief.

Pearl's mind returned to her bracelet. She thought about the moment she noticed the first missing chain link, and how she had realized it was gone after getting through the first door of The Maze. Then she thought about the second time she noticed another link missing, how it happened to be at the same time as the first, again when she returned to The Maze. Now, at the same time and place as the last two, she realized it again. *Could it be a coincidence? Or is anything really a coincidence?* At that moment, it hit her.

Each chain hanging from her wrist represented another door in The Maze, rather, another lesson to be learned. While The Maze is the dark place within her mind that represents what it physically feels like to live with depression, each chain link symbolizes a limiting belief she told herself daily. Every door she walked through welcomed her to another part of her miserable, twisted psyche. Like a pretty, pink pearl stuck inside the middle of an egotistical onion, growing layers on top of layers, her truth grew hidden, so much so that she believed she would never find herself again. While Pearl traveled through the outskirts of her subconscious mind, she found herself physically faced with her traumas, forced to really see them, feel them, and let them go. If she wanted to make it out alive, she must peel back her rotting layers, face her shadows, and ultimately, uncover her truth. Her mouth dropped open slightly and she stared at the bracelet with disbelief. *This is why he gave this to me,* she thought as she remembered Doc forcibly tying it to her wrist. *This means that I should have seven doors left.* This realization gave her hope. Pearl placed her hands into the floor and pushed herself up to standing. Her body, yet still fearful and terrified of the unknown, stood lighter on her feet. Her eyes crinkled at the corners and she could not help but smile. She knew she needed to let go, and she was ready to do so.

2

Pearl slyly sauntered further through The Maze. She kept her arms close to her sides and the hair on her skin rose tall in the cold, stagnant air. Despite the anxiety lingering throughout her body and the fear festering within, she walked forward without looking back.

This passage of The Maze stood out to Pearl differently than the ones before. Not because of the layers she had peeled off herself, but because The Maze physically looked different. The same blood-red paint covered the same, cold, concrete walls, yet this hallway appeared wider than the others. The last few times she had entered The Maze, the walls were only a bit wider than wing's span, whereas this hallway seemed to be three times that. The ceiling, too, was visible for the first time, in fact it hung so low that Pearl could just about jump up and reach for it, barely grazing the cement with the tips of her fingers. Accompanied by more dangly, flickering lightbulbs, this hall illuminated with more light than the ones prior, and it carried a stronger odor than before, too. The hallway reeked of strong mildew and decay, but no sign showed where the scent lingered from. Pearl covered her nose and mouth with the palms of her hands, holding her breath from the wretched aroma.

Pearl kept walking, relying solely on her gut instinct to guide her in the right direction. Suddenly, as she turned a left corner, she approached a metal stairwell. The spiral staircase traveled both up and down to two different stories, leaving Pearl with the decision as to which direction she would go. Immediately, she assumed going upstairs would be her best option, as below reminded her of hell. Yet, regardless of which direction she took, the lessons she needed to learn were always going to catch up with her. Even the hellish ones.

She prowled up the steps cautiously, moving slowly and on guard, as she orbited up into the unknown. The smell of rubbish faded from the air the higher she traveled, and the only thing she could hear were her own two feet stepping along the metal steps below. She held onto the cold, metal railing as she continued to climb higher. Suddenly, the railing she held onto began to clatter violently in her grip, and the stairwell rattled underneath her feet like a pack of wild animals were running up from behind her. Pearl stopped involuntarily and froze in her place.

At once, a man, just a bit older than her, came stampeding up the stairs behind her, breathing frantically and hysterically as if he was running for his life. He shoved Pearl out of his way, huffing and puffing, dripping sweat, step after step. Pearl's body flung against the metal railing, while the man continued sprinting upwards.

"Hey! Stop! Wait! Can you help me?" Pearl shouted at the running man. Alas, besides his panting breath, the man remained mute, as he continued his way up and away from Pearl. In a few seconds, the sound of his footsteps faded in the distance and the clanking metal grew still. Pearl set foot once again with speed, chasing the man up the stairs in hopes of finding help.

Pearl finally made it to the top of the spiral staircase. She shifted her gaze down a new hallway, catching sight of the running man once again. He ran frantically toward a tall, wooden door that stood alone at the end of the hall. Pearl chased after him, picking up her pace.

"Wait!" She shouted out. "Can you please help me? I need somebody!"

The man continued running away from Pearl's voice.

"Wait! Can you not hear me?" She bellowed once again. Yet, no response. He continued his pace.

The anxious man quickly approached the door and without thinking twice, he gripped the doorknob and opened it wide.

"Wait! Please!" Pearl screamed for the man. In those few seconds,

Pearl caught sight of where the door had led to. Through the door, she witnessed what appeared to be a busy city street, like New York City, with hundreds of other people walking. In an instant, the man ran inside and slammed the door behind him.

3

Pearl ran up to the door and opened it up wide, too. Yet, when she opened the door, there appeared to be no crowded, city street. Rather, this door welcomed her to a place she had already once been to. A familiar place that made her spine crawl out of her skin. She stood in disbelief, faced with the same, mysterious forest she first entered when she initially went under hypnosis. The same place she found the first door that led her to The Maze in the first place, except this time, the birch trees no longer grew lush. Rather, they appeared barren, dry to the bone, and lifeless.

"What? That doesn't make any sense! I just saw him go in here, but it wasn't... *here*." Her brows drew inwards, and she tilted her head to the side.

Before she had entered the door, she peaked her head inwards and looked all around. "What the fuck? Did I do it? Did I beat The Maze?" She took one step in, followed by the next, until the door slammed behind her on its own.

Pearl jumped at the closed door. She quickly looked over her shoulder toward the door and became uneasy to find that the door had disappeared like the ones throughout The Maze before. She shifted her gaze forward once again, and then up toward the birch trees above.

"Hello?" Pearl yelled aloud.

Nothing more than a subtle breeze whistled through the air.

"Can anyone hear me?" She shouted again.

Nothing but the wind responded back.

"Doc? Can you hear me?" She asked prudently, wondering as to why she had returned to the forest. "Did I do it? Did I make it out? Am I done?" Yet, no answer. The forest remained quiet. Pearl shifted her gaze back down in front of her. She stood there, confused, conflicted, and tense. A cold chill came over her, yet her blood boiled hot. The feeling of fear crept throughout her body once again.

"No, no—no—no. No, this cannot be happening again!" She paused for a moment, panting heavily in denial. She spun her body around quickly with anguish, as she let out a long cry for help at the top of her lungs. Then, her voice grew to herself once again. With tears in her eyes, she whispered to herself and said, "I am still in The Maze."

4

Pearl knew she had to move forward. She wiped her eyes, took a deep breath in, and did what she came here to do.

Pearl made her way along the trail with suspense, holding herself with protection and her eyes in every direction. The further she walked, the more eerie the forest grew. Clouds began to huddle toward each other, creating a thick sheet of shadowy grey. Not a crack of sunlight shined through, and as the weather grew more cold, wintry, and heavy, the small breeze creeping its way through the forest grew stronger. At first, Mother Nature danced through the branches. Her gusts of wind flowed freely, as she allowed herself to creatively express her calm, gentle beauty. Yet, Mother Nature suddenly became irritable. The storm began building, so much so, that she had no choice but to let it go. Her rhythm grew strong and almighty, transmuting into conditions of chaos. The wind smacked the sides of Pearl's face and pulled her hair in every direction.

Pearl continued to falter forward. Although her body trembled with terror and her thoughts ran a million miles per hour, she began to feel stiff. Every step she took became more ungiving than the last. This feeling grabbed her attention. She stopped for a moment and scanned her body up and down. She examined herself closely, tuning in to the areas of her being that felt physically uncomfortable. She took tiny bends in her knees and elbows and curled her fingers in and out. She sensed a tingling sensation that flowed throughout her limbs, leaving her body numb. She began to feel lethargic, tired, and drained in only a matter of minutes.

"What the hell is happening to me?" She spoke to herself.

Suddenly, a cry for help echoed throughout the forest. Pearl immediately lifted her head up and ran off the trail, making her way behind a wall of birch trees to hide. She peeked around the birch and scanned the forest before her. She saw nothing but a sea of trees, yet the helpless voice cried louder.

She focused on her surroundings with flooded, yet defensive eyes. Her breath became short and quiet, as she braced herself for the worst. Suddenly, from afar, Pearl caught sight of a person limping with hurry, making their way up the trail. She could not see who it was, at first, but as they floundered closer, she began to make out the appearance of their presence. The screaming man had a gruesome, bloody wound, leaking perpetually from the side of his skull. He had tattoos covering his arms, shaggy blonde hair, and blue eyes. Teardrops flooded his vision and rushed down his boiling red cheeks, and long with blood, sweat dripped down his face. It was clear he was running for his life. She pulled her face back behind the bark, with only one eye locked on him.

"Someone, please help me!" The man's voice screeched through the trees as he ran down the trail. Pearl remained hidden and watched from afar. As he made his way unknowingly closer to Pearl, the rhythm of her heart grew faster, and adrenaline shot through her veins. She kept her body close to the trees while gripping her hands along the bark. She waited in the shadows, as she watched the present moment unfold.

As the man ran closer toward Pearl, she moved her whole body behind the trees to take complete cover. But when she did, the man detected motion and he saw her. His eyes lit up like a Christmas tree.

"Hey! You! I need your help!" He hollered at Pearl.

Pearl squeezed her eyes shut and gritted her teeth. *Fuck,* she thought to herself. She constricted every single muscle with anticipation.

The man ran off the trail and zig-zagged through the trees, until he finally reached Pearl, who kept herself hidden behind the bark.

"You! You have to help me! You have to help me, please!" The frazzled man tripped into Pearl, grabbing her by the arms and shaking her for dear life. Fearful, Pearl immediately pulled back and pushed him off her.

"Get off of me!" She snapped back, jumping away from the bloody man.

He stood winded and desperate for help, as he stared at her with his eyes wide open. He clasped his hands together and started to beg. "You do not understand. I need to get out of here, I'm trapped. And he's going to find me."

"What happened to you? Who's going to find you?"

"He's right behind me, he's—" As the man tried to make sense of his thoughts, Pearl suddenly noticed hanging from his wrist appeared to be almost the same, exact bracelet that hung from hers. His had a single, pink pearl, like hers, yet only a few chain links remaining.

"W—wait. Where did you get that?" Pearl interrupted.

"What?"

"That!" She pointed at his bracelet.

He looked at his wrist. "The bracelet?"

Pearl nodded, frightened beyond belief.

"He gave it to me," he responded, looking Pearl deep into her eyes.

"Who did? Doc?" Pearl asked anxiously.

The man nodded. Pearl lifted her wrist and showed him her bracelet. "I have one, too."

"You're a seeker, like me." He stated, blood dripping off his chin.

The man looked away from Pearl and locked eyes on the dirt trail from where he came from. His eyebrows furrowed together and his face grew a horrific expression. He quickly covered Pearl's mouth with his bloody hand, pushed her into the trees, and huddled over her. Pearl began to squirm underneath him, yelling in the palm of his hand.

"Shhh." He whispered in her ear. "Don't speak. He's here." The man gently removed his hand from her lips. Perplexed, Pearl peeked her head around the trees once again.

Beside the trail, walking at ease up on top of a hill, had to be the biggest, most petrifying grizzly bear Pearl could have ever imagined in her wildest dreams. He stretched about ten feet long from head to tail, and he easily weighed at least two thousand pounds of pure muscle. His body walked with stealth, each muscle defined and outlined under his husky, brown fur. His mouth fell slightly open and his underbite was illuminated by the drool that dripped down from his razor-sharp teeth. He looked hungry and well-aware that dinner was near.

"Holy shit," Pearl whispered in panic. Both Pearl and the man jolted their way fully behind the trees. They huddled close together and hid quietly, squinting between the bark.

The bear paused in his place, for a moment. He lifted his nose to the sky and took a big whiff in. After he did so, his ears perked up. He knew he was close to his prey. He opened his mouth wide and let out a mighty roar, echoing the whole forest.

Pearl and the man stayed hidden behind the trees, their bodies both shaking with distress. They were overruled with dread, and apprehension shot through their veins.

"We have to get out of here. He is going to find us if we stay here," Pearl whispered to the man, her voice cracking.

"He is going to find us if he sees us move!" The man explained back.

"You got me into this mess, and I don't even know you!" Pearl snapped back.

The man looked at her as if she was stupid. He raised an eyebrow and replied, "You do realize where you are, right? You're in this door for a reason. Just like me."

Pearl froze, her eyes opened wide and her understanding grew dazed.

She realized that he was right. This was a part of whatever she needed to overcome. Two people, on two different paths, yet both ended up in the same dimension. Two mortals, both peeling the layers to find their individual truths, were looking to escape The Maze within their minds. They both looked into each other's eyes, held silence and space for a moment, and then returned to scope the bear. But when they gazed between the trunks of the trees, the bear was gone.

The man's breath grew heavier and more fast-paced than ever before. "Where did he go?" He asked aloud, as if Pearl had the answer. Still standing behind the trees, they both scanned around them, looking up and down the trail and all around the forest.

The forest fell completely quiet. Both beats of their hearts matched in a race of phobia. Suddenly, the earth's floor began to vibrate with the feeling of monstrous footsteps running up to them. A ferocious grumble began growing behind them, intensifying in volume, telling them they only had a few seconds to spare. Just then, Pearl and the man both turned their bodies around and were faced with the grizzly beast, sprinting straight toward them. Their eyes locked with his and both of their hearts dropped into their stomachs.

"Oh, fuck. Run!" They both screamed, splitting apart, and running in opposite directions.

Pearl's feet ran faster than she ever imagined they could. It was as if her body became overpowered with the adrenaline pumping through her blood. She sprinted through the forest, darting through the trees, and dodging the leafless branches.

The vibration of the beast's feet faded quickly from underneath hers. As she ran, she quickly glanced over her left shoulder. When she did, she noticed the bear's backside running away from her, and toward the limping, bloody man.

Pearl came to a halt and ran behind another tall, lifeless birch tree. As she caught up with her breath, she peeked her eyes over and watched the hunt.

Pearl observed the man running for his life, trying to catch his breath with every step he took. Woefully, the grizzly suddenly stood up on his back legs, standing at about ten feet tall. He let out a mighty roar, lifted one paw, and swatted the man like a fly, flinging him about twenty feet forward and face first into the dirt. In that instant, the bear ran over to the man and landed his briskly body on top of him, crushing his claws into his face as he ripped him to shreds. His sounds of screaming terror echoed throughout the forest and his eyes flooded with pain. The bear swiped the man's face repetitively, gashing and digging into his head and body. Blood gushed out of him like a rapid river of insides. The man immediately left his body. He grew lifeless.

Pearl's hands instinctively covered her mouth with disbelief as she gasped for a breath. She had been a witness to a cruel, horrific massacre. Her eyes opened wide, blankly staring at the killer. Like a gruesome car crash, she could not help but watch.

The bear chomped into the man's body, his teeth and lips dripping fresh blood. After he finished his meal, the bear turned his body toward Pearl's direction and instantaneously locked eyes with hers. There they stood, with space in between them. The bear, glaring at Pearl, tilted his head down and back up. With a single grunt, the bear turned back into the depths of the forest, gifting Pearl mercy. It was as if the bear had been programmed to spare Pearl, like The Maze had a different plan in store for her. Although she and the man met in that same door, they each walked on their own journeys, with their own lessons to be learned.

5

Pearl ran away from the scene, going wherever direction her feet took her. In a state of panic and traumatized at the sight of a man being eaten alive right before her eyes, she could hardly even think, let alone process where to go next. Everywhere she turned looked the same, perceiving nothing but thousands of white, lifeless trees. Sweat leaked from her pores and her heart pounded rapidly against her chest.

She ran for about five more minutes through the forest, until the peculiar sensation of stiffness began to creep through her body once again. Her sprinting turned into running, her running morphed into a jog, until suddenly, she could move no more than a lumber.

She stepped slowly, her body growing more and more lethargic and weak. She had no clue why, and she questioned herself and everything around her. As she stepped forward, she began to clench her hands into fists once again, doing everything in her power to keep them energized.

With her attention focused on her body, Pearl suddenly tripped over her feet, losing control of herself. Her body fell forward, and she landed onto her hands and knees. When she landed, she noticed her palms began to sink into the earth below her. She pulled one hand up and off the ground using all her strength. As she did, her other hand sunk deeper down, followed by her knees and feet. She quickly looked all around her body and became aware that she had fallen into an absorbing puddle of quicksand. The earth swallowed her hands, her wrists, and her elbows, followed by her knees, her shins, and thighs. It pulled her down, as if she no longer had any control of herself. Whatever she did, and no matter how hard she fought, the forces fought harder. She felt as if the world was swallowing her whole. Pearl continued to fight, yet her body felt tired, rigid, and weak. In fact, she felt the same as if she were at home in the real world, lost in her body and mind, unmotivated to get up out of bed. No matter how much rest she had gotten the night before, she felt simply drained with little to no life. As the quicksand swallowed her whole, she felt no different than she did when she suffered with depression, every day of her life.

"Somebody help me!" She screamed out loud. Her body sunk halfway down into the sand, pulling her deeper and faster. She jolted back and forth, still fighting with every ounce of energy she had left. Suddenly,

Pearl shifted her gaze up in front of her and noticed the vicious grizzly bear walking up to her. Pearl's breath became rapid, as she found herself breathless with what she believed were the last few breaths of her life. The beast watched her with interest, as if her misery and suffering were more entertaining for him than eating her up. He sat his bottom down next to her and watched her sink, his mouth slightly fallen as if he were smiling.

Pearl's body became stiffer, weaker, and incapable to move. The sand pulled her down, constricting itself over her. She screamed at the top of her lungs until her head was the last to be swallowed. With the bear's eyes locked on Pearls, she took one final breath, until the earth gulped. Everything went black.

# Door #5
# I Am Anxious

1

Life struck back into her body for the fifth time. She awoke abruptly with a gasp of breath, filling her lungs with tremendous space. Her body shot up and away from the floor as if she had been revived from the dead. Her eyes jolted open, as she blinked them rapidly to focus. Alas, her clouded eyes revealed the red walls and concrete floors of The Maze once again. She smacked her chest with both of her hands and let out a ridiculous cough, like life itself was too big to swallow. Finally, she got her breath somewhat under control. Rooted down into her sit bones, she rubbed her eyes clean, rolled her shoulders back, then pushed herself up to standing. Suddenly, it hit her. Her eyes glossed over while the world became clearer with her next breath.

The familiar feeling in the pit of her stomach began to fade away: the feeling of the world swallowing her whole. She felt steady on her feet, and it was as if the floor underneath her had finally stopped swaying. Her arms, her legs, her fingers, and her toes began to tingle as the overwhelming sensation swept over her being. She felt tortured, yet she felt herself standing lighter than ever before. Pearl had realized that it was not the world that was swallowing her all these years, rather, it was simply her own reality. She was not the center of the world—she most certainly was not that special—and this target she believed to be painted on her back really was a façade she had imagined all along. Although she had faced incredible hardships throughout her life, her eternal suffering was not a product of the world, the cosmos, the Universe, God, or anything else outside of her. This target was created by the false narrative she told herself on a daily, furthering the victim mentality she had come to know and believe. She felt as if the world craved to eat her alive, and so it did when she convinced herself it was true. However, in this moment, instead of believing the world was out to get her, she felt one with her Self, Source, the world, and life all around. She knew that the only way for her to continue peeling the rotten layers was to step foot into the discomfort, and the further she traveled through The Maze, the more uncomfortable her journey would become. And despite the many more lessons she needed to learn, she felt revived, alive, and grateful for the ride. She took a conscious, deep breath in, and a deeper breath out, bringing her attention to the chain links on her bracelet.

*One, two, three, four, five, six,* she counted in her head. Her smile grew wide and her eyes began to twinkle under the dim, hanging light-bulbs. *I have a chance,* she thought to herself. *I can do this.*

2

Despite every step feeling lighter than before, anxiety still crawled over her skin and throughout every inch of her body. Regardless of the new lessons she had learned and the ego deaths she had faced within the walls of The Maze, she knew one thing for sure: The Maze was a hellish, torture chamber. The energy felt eerie, heavy, and dark, and fear crept throughout her mind and body with every step she took. She wanted nothing more than to get out of this place, and she was determined to unravel whatever stood in her way.

Pearl traveled through The Maze for about thirty minutes or so, turning corners and venturing into new, uncharted halls. Eventually, she found herself standing in another corridor. However, this time, the corridor branched out into three different halls. One went to the left, one went to the right, and one extended straight out in front of her.

She stood there, examining each hallway and their minimal differences. Just like the rest of The Maze, the halls before her were red, narrow, and constructed of concrete. The ceilings extended so high that she could not even see the top, and each path appeared barely dimmed with light. Pearl found it difficult to decide which direction to choose, as they all looked practically the same. She scanned her options one last time, until, on a whim, she chose the path that trekked dead ahead, down the middle hall.

Pearl tiptoed ahead, making her way further down the hall. As she moved deeper into the unknown, the sound of footsteps began echoing throughout The Maze, as if more than one person were following from behind. Pearl stopped in her tracks with her heart beating out of her chest. She glanced over her right shoulder, more than terrified to see what it could be. She saw nothing but an empty hall that stretched back into the darkness. *What was that?* She thought to herself.

She shifted her gaze back forward. About twenty feet ahead at the end of the hall appeared to be two young girls, standing ominously still. One stood tall, about five foot eight inches. She had thin, perfectly straight, sun-kissed blonde hair that rested over her chest. Her cheeks were red and rosy, and she had an eerily wide smile that stretched ear to ear. The other girl stood about five feet tall. She had thick, short brown hair that looked perfectly groomed, and mesmerizing, sinful eyes that squinted with her devious smile. One would believe the two of them had never seen light before; with pasty, translucent, white skin. Parts of them seemed to be cracking like porcelain dolls. They both had big, dark circles under their eyes, and they each wore old, polka dotted dresses that appeared dirty, tattered, and torn at the seams. From the outside, they looked to be human, however, something about them had an otherworldly, supernatural presence. They were mysterious, deluded, and predictably up to no good, and the intensity made Pearl's skin crawl.

The two of them stood side by side each other at the end of the hall, with forceful, wicked smiles painted across their faces. They stared through Pearl, laughing at her expense, as if they knew something bad was about to happen.

Pearl stared back at the two with nothing but fear in her eyes. Her breath was involuntarily short, while every strand of hair stretched up and off of her skin. Anxiety swept over her once again.

The girls continued to stare back, giggling to one another. Then, the brunette tapped the blonde's shoulder, whispered into her ear, and then suddenly, they made a run for it around the corner, further down the hall.

Pearl's body remained frozen. Her chest puffed in and out repeatedly like she could not catch a decent breath, and her shoulders hovered right underneath her earlobes. As the voices of the giggling girls faded in the air, Pearl took a single step back behind her, followed by another one, until she made a run for it, still locking eyes in the direction the girls had run. Out of nowhere and with only a few more steps, Pearl found herself running into a dead end, straight into the cement, blood-red wall. She placed both hands on the wall, feeling around it like it had a secret way of getting through. Alas, it was like the hall she had just come through was never there in the first place, and rather than having an option to turn back around, she was forced to move forward. So, she turned back around, took a conscious, deep breath in and a deeper breath out, and began making her way down her original path, following the running, otherworldly girls.

Pearl lumbered forward. She held onto her crossed arms and kept her chin low, tucked into her chest. As she approached a turn in the hall, she noticed a small beam of light coming from around the corner. Initially, Pearl peeked her head around the corner, only to find that the beam of light came from an individual lightbulb that hung on a measly extension cord from the never-ending ceiling. It flickered in the dark, like it had been slightly unscrewed. Below the light stood a door that had a static print like a broken television painted all over it, and a black, porcelain doorknob.

Before moving forward, she looked over her shoulder for a moment once again. However, what she noticed only frightened her more. The dead end that stood behind her appeared to be closer than it was the last time she looked back. Pearl gasped for a breath and raised both eyebrows. Anxiety pulsed through her heart.

Pearl shifted her gaze back forward, this time noticing that the static painted door she just discovered stood closer than it did a few seconds ago, too. *What the fuck?* She thought to herself.

She shifted her gaze over her shoulder another time, only to find that the red, cement wall had moved even closer. She shot a glance toward the static door one last time. This time, the door had come from around the corner of the corridor and now stood an inch from her nose. It was as if Pearl was standing in a shrinking box that had only one way out. As both ends of the hallway moved closer and closer with every glance, and with only a small space left for her to stand in before she was smashed in between the walls, she had no choice but to open the door and run inside. She grabbed ahold of the porcelain doorknob, turned it rapidly to the right, and threw herself through.

Pearl's eyes stayed glued shut as she anticipated what she had just walked into. She clenched her teeth, along with every muscle in her body, as she took her first steps through her fifth door of The Maze.

3

As she made her way inside, the door closed behind her on its own. Gradually, Pearl peeled her eyes open, opening them wide in disbelief.

The door brought her into what appeared to be an awfully outdated toy shop, at least a century or two old. The first thing that caught Pearl's eye were the hundreds of eyes of porcelain dolls, stuffed dolls, and puppets resting along the shelves on top of shelves. The shelves were dusty and made of glass, and they hung against termite-infested wood panels, chipping away like the whole building was about to collapse any minute. Even the wood floor below, creaking from Pearl standing still, appeared unstable, unsupported, and distrusting. *One wrong move in here and I am plummeting through the floor and down to hell,* she thought. *Oh wait, I'm already here.*

In one corner of the room sat a rugged, wooden desk, also infested with termites, and a painfully uncomfortable looking chair beside it. On top of the desk, rested puppet strings, ceramic clay, googly eyes and other toy scraps and tools, as well as a flickering lantern, barely lighting the space. To the right, Pearl noticed an entry to another room. It had no door, rather it had an old, stained sheet hanging in the doorframe, obstructing her vision to see what hid on the other side. Pearl scanned the rest of the room, bringing awareness to her new, distressing surroundings.

She brought her attention back toward the creepy dolls. There were so many of them, mostly porcelain and puppets, encircling her. Some were damaged, missing pieces of their arms or face, some missing one or both eyes. Yet, one thing Pearl noticed they had in common was that they were all staring in Pearl's direction, even the blind ones. Pearl's involuntary breath had become so short and nervous, that she had to remind herself to breathe.

Pearl felt anxious beyond belief. Without even thinking, her feet backed up to the fifth door of The Maze. Instead of pressing her back into the door, she found herself up against another wall lined with glass shelves holding at least a hundred more ceramic dolls looking down at her. The entrance to this hoarded doll house was just that. It was an entry, not an escape. The door vanished into thin air and left her stranded like the doors before.

Her throat gulped as if it were swallowing a dry pill. Her nervous, shaky hands pushed herself away from the glass shelves, while she looked up at the hundreds of eyes glaring down at her. Her lips quivered as she tried to catch her breath. With the softest of steps, the rotting wood creaked loudly underneath her feet, as she slowly continued to step back to the middle of the room.

Pearl rooted her feet down into the ground. She rotated her head from side to side, observing each doll and their unsettling, blood-curdling differences. Something about porcelain dolls made Pearl feel uncomfortable in her own skin, even more so than she already felt, and despite the inanimate nature of the dolls, she could feel real, lifelike eyes on her. She knew she was not alone.

Suddenly, a loud crash shot from the other room behind the dirty, white sheet. Pearl jumped up, her body jolting like a bolt of lightning struck through her veins. She rooted her feet into the floor, frozen in her tracks, while her gaze shifted over to the direction of the unknown noise.

Another crash shocked through the room, this time louder than before. Suddenly, right before her eyes, a ball of yarn came rolling out from the other room and underneath the sheet. It rolled nimbly toward her, until it knocked into the side of her right foot and bounced off. She stared down at the ball of yarn, not making any sudden movements.

Amid the doubtful circumstances, the energy in the room became prominent. The ball of yarn began rocking unsteadily back and forth on its own besides her feet. Suddenly, a Huntsman spider bigger than her head reached one leg out, then two, then three before her eyes.

Pearl shrieked at the top of her lungs. Without thinking twice, she kicked the ball of yarn the second she saw the spider's legs, striking it into one of the glass shelves. The spider infested ball of yarn bounced into the face of a one-legged porcelain doll, knocking it off the shelf and shattering her into a thousand pieces. Pearl clenched her eyes shut and gritted her teeth, in hopes of not making a sound amongst the shattering ceramic before her. When she peeled her eyes back, she noticed the head of the shattered doll was the only thing intact. It lied on the wood floor, and its eyes remained locked on Pearl's.

Pearl's stomach churned rapidly, and for a second, she even believed she would throw up. Meanwhile, she heard a muffled voice come from the other room. She knew it was a man's voice. It had a deep, gravely tone to it. Although it was too far away to make sense of the words being spoken, it was close enough to convince Pearl to hide.

Immediately, she ran over to the old, wooden desk. She got down on her knees, curled up into a ball, and hid underneath the desk. She pulled the chair in front of her, camouflaging herself even more, while holding her anxious breath in. Quickly, the voice grew louder, and his words became clearer.

"What was that? Marleen, did ya' hear that?" The voice spoke with a Southern accent.

Pearl remained silent, still holding her breath.

"Who's out here!? I know someone's out here!" The voice yelled again.

The wood floor began to creak. From the other side of the hanging sheet, walked out an abnormally tall—about seven-foot—hunched, slender man. He wore a red-checkered flannel that was buttoned all the way up to his neck, and he had brown, torn-up pants that dragged underneath his bare feet. His skin appeared grey and sagged greatly, and the small number of teeth he did have remaining were rotting from the inside out.

"How did you get here?" He asked aloud, as he approached the smashed porcelain doll lying hopelessly on the floor. He picked up the doll's head and looked into its eyes. "Who did this to yah?" The man looked up and scanned the room, his eyes squinting with focus. Pearl remained still and silent. She watched his feet pace back and forth from underneath the desk. "I know someone is in here," he stated firmly.

A tear rolled down Pearl's cheek. The man's feet dragged over the splintered floorboards and toward the wooden desk, making his way so close by her that all she could see were his grimy, repulsive, boiled covered, toe-jammed filled feet. His toenails were as long as acrylic nails, and between his left big toe and second toe, a yellow maggot crawled up and out of his crusted skin, making its way down into the floor below.

She held her breath and covered her mouth even tighter, gagging on her own tongue.

"I know you are here," he spoke with a threateningly low tone. Suddenly, a woman's voice shouted from the other room.

"Grim!"

"What!?"

"Did you get ahold of the last contestant? What's her name again?"

"I don't know, Marleen, yah gotta check the book!" The man bowlegged his way toward the back room with the porcelain doll's head in his hand.

Pearl remained still beneath the desk, meanwhile listening to the voices of the strange man and woman become muffled once again. *There must be a way out of here,* Pearl thought to herself. *I cannot be stuck here, there is no way. There must be a door somewhere.*

Pearl looked through the wooden chair in hopes of finding a way out. Suddenly, she heard the pitter-patter of tiny steps running throughout the room. The beat of her heart danced faster while her anxiety continued to fester beneath her skin.

Suddenly, the pitter-patter sound tapped up above her head and along the wooden desk, almost as if someone were drumming their fingers on top of the table. But instead, from the edge of the table, crawled the massive Huntsman spider, running like it had a fire under its ass, toward Pearl. She jolted, smacking the top of her skull against the desk, while letting out a horrendous yelp, forgetting that she was hiding for her life. Pearl kicked out the chair and flung her body from hiding.

"Did you hear that?" The woman's voice asked.

"She's here." The man spoke back.

4

Pearl stopped in her tracks. She looked toward the other room and past the sheet, until she started to panic. She looked left, right, and left again, forward, back, and forward once more. She shuffled to the front left corner of the room like the whole world was shrinking before her. She cornered herself, shaking out of her skin with agonizing anticipation. She could not even imagine what was about to happen.

The floor began to vibrate below her feet. From the uncharted room, footsteps started stomping toward Pearl. With every step growing louder and louder, she stood ready to fight, considering flight was not an option. Long, skeletal fingers curled around the sheet and pulled it back. In front of her stood the barefooted man with maggots crawling out from all over his skin. He stared into Pearl's eyes like he had finally found what he had been forever in search of.

"You're here," he said. "You've had everyone waitin' for the longest time. Pretty rude, don't yah think?"

Pearl stared back at him, not saying a word.

He looked down at the shattered body of the porcelain doll and then back to Pearl. "I reckon you did that?"

She continued to freeze over.

"Huh," the man snickered to himself, looking down at the doll's head in his hand. "You know, you're not going to get yourself very far if you stay quiet like you are. I know you here broke that doll, and I want to hear yah admit it."

Pearl stared at the man with tears overflowing her eyes. Her lips quivered as if she wanted to say something, but she could not find the words.

He walked up to her, practically hovering over her body. "Say it, or you'll best regret ever stepping foot in here."

*I already do,* she thought. "I broke it. I'm—I'm sorry, it was an accident." She admitted.

He raised an eyebrow, squinted his eyes at hers, and took a step back. Out of the other room, a woman, rather, a bare to the bone woman, came moseying on out. She wore a blue, dragging cloak that covered everything from the crown of her head, to the tips of her toes, and she carried a novel in her hand, flailing it in the air.

"Here it is, Grim. You gotta' look with your eyes, not your mouth, yah know." Her voice cracked like a smoker's. She opened the book and began flipping through the pages. Her eyes skimmed the words below her and her index finger followed. "Ah, yes. Here we go. Her name is Pearl."

Pearl's cheeks burned hot and her temples dripped with sweat, yet she kept a powerful persona. She shifted her gaze between the two several times.

"Is this her?" The woman continued.

"Yeah, this is her." The man spoke low through his gritting teeth. "You know, it's pretty selfish to keep people waiting, Pearl. And let me tell you, we have all been waiting for you for a long-ass time. You'll be getting yours, trust me."

Pearl stayed silent, as she tried to catch up to her racing thoughts.

The man shook his head to the side. "Let's go." The man and woman headed back toward the room while Pearl remained rooted. The man engulfed with rage and stopped in his place. With his back still facing Pearl, he said, "Why aren't yah comin'? You don't wanna play the hard way, do yah?"

Pearl had already played the hard way. In fact, she could not imagine what the easy way to play would look like in The Maze. *Was there even such a thing?* She wondered doubtfully. With everything she had learned in The Maze thus far, she knew that the best way to get through was to comply with whatever the door threw her way. She learned that lesson the hardest way. So, she followed.

5

They pulled the dirty sheet aside and walked into the room. Just like the first room, the floor, the walls, and the ceiling were made of termite-infested wood. Off to the left stood a rustic bureau with another porcelain doll sitting on top, polished and untouched. It had both of its arms and legs, and despite its perfect presence compared to the dolls before, they all had one thing in common. Its eyes locked on Pearl's from the moment she walked in.

Against the back wall stood an unnerving contraption she had never seen before. It had a wooden floor base, with two shackles locked into place. On the back of the board and behind the chains stood a tall, wooden post with a headlock attached to it at the top, and about ten feet above the apparatus hung what looked like a massive operating cross for a toy puppet. It had four puppet-looking strings that hung so thick, they could have been rope, and the operating cross dangled from a metal rolling track that carved through the ceiling. The track ran along the ceiling from above the device, all the way across the room and into another door that solely stood against the right wall. Nothing about this room felt safe or admirable. Pearl gulped as she walked further inside.

The man led Pearl further into the room. Meanwhile, the other woman was nowhere to be found. *She must have gone through this other door,* Pearl thought to herself. She could only imagine what it led to.

The man walked over to the apparatus, inviting Pearl to follow.

"Here it is," he said, introducing Pearl to the machine with his arms out wide.

"Wha—what is this?" She asked anxiously, holding onto opposite elbows.

"This is the *Puppet Master.* Now, come on, you're already late. Everyone is waitin' on you. Step up here." He pointed at the wooden floor base.

Pearl took a deep breath in through her nose, and a rich exhale out of her mouth. A thought passed through her mind about all the reasons she should not step onto the plank. But she reminded herself all the reasons that she should, and those most certainly outweighed the ones not to. *I've already made it this far into The Maze,* she thought. *I can't turn back now.* No matter how anxious she felt in the moment, she stepped up to the board, turned around, and stood against the wooden pole.

First, the man handcuffed Pearl from behind, locking her to the wooden post. Next, he locked her feet into the floor, securing the shackles around her ankles tight, and then finally, he strapped her head into the headlock. She felt beyond petrified and wanted to keep her eyes closed shut, yet, she did not bare to blink. Her skin leaked warm sweat and her heart pounded hard.

"What are you going to do to me?"

The man looked at her deeply with his wicked eyes. Without saying a word, he stepped behind the machine. He reached up for the operating cross, or the *Puppet Master* as he called it, and untangled the four, dangling ropes. Each rope tied to its own limb. One rope tied to her right wrist, one tied to her left wrist, one tied to her right ankle, and finally, the last rope tied to her left ankle. He suited her up, double-checking each knot to make sure they were tied tightly. They were. She could barely turn her wrist or ankles, and the circulation in her hands and feet began to cut back. Within a few short moments, she could no longer feel her fingers or her toes. After completion, he unbuckled the headlock, unlocked the handcuffs, and released the shackles from her ankles. He took a step back, looked her up and down, and could not help but flash a malicious grin.

"She's ready," he said quietly to himself, yet loud enough for Pearl to hear.

He walked over to the bureau and slid the porcelain to the side. Against the wall behind the doll hung a small, red switch. He pointed his index finger up toward the switch as his smile slithered deeper from cheek to cheek. He looked back at Pearl once more.

"You ready?"

With little to no confidence, Pearl nodded.

He flipped the switch. Suddenly, the *Puppet Master* ignited like a revved-up engine. It began to take shape, lifting one side higher than the other. Pearl's right hand raised tall, followed by her left foot. Then, the machine switched arms and legs. Her right hand and left foot lowered, while her left hand and right foot went up in the air.

"Just a few more seconds before we move forward. We want to make sure this thing is warmed up." The man continued watching the operating cross make all its adjustments above Pearl.

Pearl shifted her gaze up toward the cross. It tilted left, right, up, down, and side to side, just like a hand controlling a string puppet. Her limbs followed closely behind.

"Perfect. It's ready. Let's go," the man declared.

Pearl had no choice. She found herself hooked onto a human controlling device, as if she were a life size puppet on strings with zero control over her own body.

Suddenly, the machine jolted, then began rolling forward on its track, walking Pearl like a dog. One foot after another after another, all dictated by the *Puppet Master*. It led her forward, making its way toward the peculiar door that the woman must have gone through.

Before Pearl knew it, she became face to face with the unopened door.

"Make me look good out there, yah hear me?" The man ordered.

Pearl glanced over to the man, furrowed her brows, then looked back at the door, swallowing her anxiety. The man reached for the doorknob, turned it forcefully, and swung the door open wide for Pearl. She gasped.

6

Pearl was hit with the screams and cheers of a stadium full of baseball fans who just watched the ball get struck out of the park. The door opened into a massive amphitheater, like the size of a football field, with a roof overhead. There were tens of thousands of screaming fans standing up and out of their seats. They all faced Pearl, as if they had been waiting for this moment all their lives. They cheered, pounded their fists in the air, and whistled at her like wild animals. All eyes were glued on her. She was the ball that had been struck out of the park.

In front of Pearl rested a small, wooden beam that had a tight-rope stretching all the way to another unopened door that stood on the opposite side of the amphitheater. Above her continued the metal track that controlled the *Puppet Master*, and it extended to the other door, too. Underneath the tightrope, she noticed a pool of maggots, centipedes, and spiders of all kinds. There were cockroaches and rats scurrying all around, and some of the world's deadliest snakes slithering about. There appeared to be so much gruesome life underneath her that she could not see a speck of floor.

"You have let anxiety control you all of your life, like the puppet you are. Here, it is all worth it." The man said to Pearl. He pushed her out the door and onto the beam.

She swallowed again, as she tripped up to the step. She peered down toward the other end of the tightrope, slowly walking her eyes toward the tops of her feet. She could not help but notice how high up she stood. Three hundred, maybe four hundred feet high, she thought. If she fell, it would be high enough to kill her faster than the vermin underneath her ever would. Yet, the thought of her dead body being attacked and eaten away while almost a hundred thousand screaming lunatics watched admirably felt more disturbing than the fall itself. She had no choice.

"Go!" "Faster!" "Hurry up, bitch!" "Walk!" "Do it!" The crowd shouted at Pearl.

Suddenly, the operating cross hanging above her head began to move forward, pulling her with it. For a moment, she looked back at the gruesome man behind her. His wicked smile slithered deeper across his face, and his eyes squinted back at hers. She shifted her gaze back forward and began her balancing act.

Her right foot lifted and stepped onto the tightrope, followed by her left. The beginning felt not too challenging, considering she was supported by the rope. But as the operating cross rolled forward, without hesitation, it forced her to follow. The further she walked, the tighter the tightrope became.

Pearl stepped slowly, like a baby learning how to walk for the first time. The machine controlled her legs, stepping them forward one at a time, and it controlled her arms, pulling them up with every alternating step. Like a monkey on a dance floor, she gave into the control. She was a puppet of her own anxiety.

Halfway she walked, in the center of the stadium. Really, she did not have much to do except let the strings do the work. However, as she continued forward like a ragdoll, and between the screams and hollers of the ever so entertained audience, a small tearing noise began to ring through her ear.

Her gaze shifted up toward the *Puppet Master*. Between her and the rolling machine, she noticed the rope hooked onto her right foot begin to tear slightly. Her eyes pierced open and adrenaline shot through her veins. She looked around frantically while maintaining her pace. Sweat began to drip down her temple and every muscle in her body grew tense.

Quickly, the slight tear quickly grew into a big rip. Pearl's focus became obscured. She could not think of anything other than her falling to her death. Steadily, she tried turning her head back toward the man that hooked her to the abrasive machine.

"Hey! It's ripping! The rope is ripping!" She shouted to him. Yet, by the time she turned her head around enough to see where he once stood, she realized he, and the door she had come through, had disappeared.

She looked back up toward the ripping rope and saw that it was only hanging by a thread, until suddenly, it snapped in two.

Anxiety shot through her body like a bullet. She tried her best to remain calm, even though she was screaming on the inside. There were three ropes still tied to her, one on her left ankle, and the other two on each wrist. *Don't panic,* she thought to herself. *Just keep walking and follow the machine. I'm almost there.*

She made it about three-quarters of the way there, until the sound of tearing reached her ear once again. Pearl looked up rapidly. It appeared to be the rope tied to her left ankle distracting her with sound. *Great,* she thought. She acknowledged that this rope had probably only a minute more before snapping. She shifted her gaze back to center, and said to herself, "You can do it. You're almost there." However, in thirty short seconds, the rope snapped. There she stood, hundreds of feet up in the sky, surrounded by thousands of screaming prisoners and creatures, walking on her own with only her hands tied and controlled. She felt unbalanced and anxious in her own body. She wanted to stop, but the *Puppet Master* said otherwise.

The machine continued rolling forward toward the other door. Pearl followed along since her hands were still captive. She focused on her feet, moving slowly with every step she took. *Heel-toe, heel-toe, heel-toe, heel-toe.*

In the midst of the chaos around her, Pearl took a moment and scanned the audience. She stared ominously at the thousands of eyes that stared back at her. As she observed the crowd, two familiar faces caught her eyes. The living dead girls dressed in polka dot dresses, the same ones she saw in The Maze before she had entered the fifth door, sat in the crowd smiling, laughing, and pointing at Pearl. The sight of those girls made Pearl cringe.

Pearl glanced back ahead. She focused her attention down onto her feet, breaking more than a sweat with every step she took. *Heel, toe, heel, toe, heel, toe...*she thought to herself.

She could practically taste the end of the zipline. The closer she got, the clearer the unopened door became to her. *Only a few more steps,* she thought to herself. She shifted her gaze up toward the door, and with a confident breath, the door suddenly opened wide before her. There he stood, the little boy with a thousand teeth, between the door frame. His goat eyes were opened wide and he flashed his rows of baby fangs at Pearl. He waved at her, giggling wickedly to himself.

Suddenly, her sense of balance had vanished as her anxiety began to boil. Pearl tripped over her feet, bouncing along the tightrope while her hands remained captive. With the fumbles and tumbles of her balancing act, her feet left the tightrope. Her fall was quickly caught by the knots around her wrists. She swung off from the zipline and hung desperately from her wrists, hanging with nothing below her feet. Panic overruled her. She flailed her body, kicking her feet back and forth as she screamed at the top of her lungs. In those few seconds of chaos, the rope tied to her left wrist snapped under pressure. The snap set Pearl swinging, spinning in circles so quickly that she couldn't see a thing. However, she could hear the chanting crowd grow louder, more amplified. Her right hand continued to dangle from the operating cross, dragging her even closer to the boy. Pearl reached up toward the cross with her left hand to try to carry herself up. Yet, Pearl's weight, although light, grew too heavy for the single rope to handle. The fourth and final rope snapped, no longer assisting Pearl, and released her wrist. She fell from the cross, yet as gravity took her down, she managed to hook her right knee onto the tightrope and catch her disastrous fall. The audience cheered louder.

Pearl grasped onto the tight rope with both hands, keeping her right knee still hooked on. Upside down, she crawled toward the ledge, still fighting for her life. She reached her right hand up to the beam, curled her fingers over and gripped it, until suddenly, the little boy walked up to her, and smiled at her with his demonic, goat-like eyes. Suddenly, he stepped his foot onto her hands, crushing her fingers like he was crushing a bug. Pearl screeched in pain, and in an instant, she let go of the ledge, the zipline, and her chance. The crowd went wild.

# Door #6
# I Am Numb

## 1

Her eyes lit up like an electric sky. As though she were shocked back to life, her back shot up and off the floor. Breath flooded her lungs, and life rapidly returned to the rest of her being. Her fingers and toes tingled intensely and the hair on her skin shot up toward the never-ending ceiling. Her pupils dilated like a dark, black pool and she choked on another layer of her awakening. She did not feel ready for it, though, she never would.

For so many years of Pearl's young life, anxiety hid in her shadows, following her every which way and controlling her like a puppet. While she sat there, recollecting her breath in the The Maze for the sixth time, she felt the pit in her stomach, despite its depths, empty its anxious sensations and flood with light. As she peeled the onion even further, she became mindful of the anxiety that ate at her from the inside out every day. Anxiety stems from a lack of presence. Unintentionally, Pearl spent about every moment of her depressed life gripping tightly onto the past, or constantly wondering of what ifs for the future. When one gets caught up with anxiety, they submit to the monkey mind, and permit time to pass them by. Time is invaluable and this moment, the only moment one truly has, is beyond precious. Life is meant to be enjoyed in the moment, while taking the lessons from one's past with them forever, constantly growing, learning, and shedding layers that hold them back from their best version of themselves. One must let go of the past in order to move forward, yet one must also let go of the unknown future, for it is never promised. Waking up tomorrow is not guaranteed, in fact, walking down another hallway of The Maze is not even certain, yet the uncertainty should never keep one confined in a single spot. Although this new sense of presence poured over her, she understood that in order to see her Self clearly, she would have to do more than uncover the root of anxiety. While anxiety encouraged the monkey mind to run wild, the monkey mind did not need anxiety's permission to run even wilder. To further uncover her truth, Pearl must unmask her shadows, bring them to the surface, become aware of the mental chatter, and release all of the fear from within her. Pearl was more than willing to do whatever it took to do so. She would be nobody's puppet. Instead, she would be the Puppet Master. Pearl took a deep breath in, embracing the presence the moment had to offer, and a deeper breath out.

With this new set of lenses, she shifted her gaze down at the chain links hanging from her wrist. She counted aloud.

"One, two, three, four, five…" She whispered to herself, nodding at her victory thus far. "One less than last time. One step closer." She smiled.

Pearl pushed herself up onto her feet, and began making her way back down The Maze. This time, with her strings untied.

2

This part of The Maze stretched long out in front of her. More red walls, a ceiling that her eyes could not see, and chilling air that lingered throughout. Nothing new. Her guard remained up, her eyes remained focused, and she skulked with intention, hoping for the best, yet preparing for the worst.

She made her way deeper into The Maze. Eventually, the end of the hall approached quickly. She could see a dead end not too much farther ahead, yet not a single door standing in sight.

"What the hell?" Pearl said quietly to herself. She raised an eyebrow and squinted her eyes to get a better look, doubting her vision. Yet, her eyes spoke with truth. She looked over her shoulder and noticed the hall stretch far back from behind her. She knew she did not pass a single door. *I think?* She thought with doubt. *No, I didn't pass any doors, I would remember that.* Pearl turned her head back forward. She continued walking toward the dead end just to be sure there was nothing more. And it is a good thing she did, too.

As she approached the end of the hall, she noticed red, wood pallets in front of her, about three feet wide and three feet long, nailed into the floor. They were dilapidated and rotten, like they had withstood ferocious waves of water that had once flooded The Maze. Pearl stared, wide-eyed and curious as to why they were there.

She tapped the wood with her shoes. It felt hollow underneath. *Probably covering a hole,* she thought. As she examined the wood, suddenly, the sound of running footsteps, followed by the giggles of a small child, echoed the hall behind her. *The boy with a thousand teeth,* she thought. *He found me.*

Her skin crawled like a spider up a wall. Pearl shot a glance behind her, looking up and down the hallway immediately. Still, nothing but an empty hall. She gulped, breathing through her anxious sensations.

She slowly shifted her gaze back down toward the wood pallets, curious as to what could be underneath that would be restricting her access. Immediately, while her eyes were gazed down, the sound of running footsteps evolved into sprinting, and Pearl stood at the finish line. The footsteps darted through the hallway, increasing louder and louder the closer they got to her. The laughter of a devious child echoed once again, growing only more ferocious with the sprinting steps.

Pearl immediately turned around and looked up once again, startled. She faltered backwards, overridden with fear. Suddenly, her heel caught the edge of one of the pallets, causing her to stumble even harder. Her foot punched a hole through the tattered debris and she fell ass-first into the floor. Silence swept through the hall once again.

Pearl started to panic. She looked up and down the hall first; nothing stood in her path. Relieved, she looked down at her feet, acknowledged the scrapes along the back of her shoe, then gazed toward the nailed wood. She pulled her foot out from the wood, crossed her ankles, placed her hands out in front of her, and made her way to all fours. Pearl peered through the busted hole to see what hid underneath.

Under the wood pallets appeared darkness, she could not see a thing but black below her. As she looked through, the eerie footsteps raced through the hall once again. Pearl looked up and down the hall from which she had just come; toward the dead end, and then back toward the pallets. She sat back on her butt, lifted her legs up, and began bashing both heels into the wood. As the footsteps grew louder and giggles began taunting once again, with all her might, Pearl busted through the pallets. She peeled back fragments and stomped the termite infested wood until she made enough space to jump through. Then, without thinking twice, she jumped into the darkness.

3

Silence swept over her once again. She stood underneath the busted floorboards and tried to examine her new surroundings, but it was pitch black and she couldn't see a thing. Yet, in the distance, she heard the subtle sounds of beats, maybe House music, bumping and vibrating loudly. She listened closer.

With her new, shifted paradigm, and with a conscious breath in and out, she made her way forward with only the sound of music to guide her there. She placed her hands out in front of her and blindly walked ahead.

As she slinked further, the music bumped louder. Meanwhile, a faded light began to make shape up ahead. The dim light outlined the room around it. She found herself walking down another hall of The Maze, surrounded by the same red walls that were cracked throughout, yet this hall had a ceiling hanging above at almost six feet high, barely grazing over Pearl's head as she moved. She continued forward.

Step by step, she finally reached the hazy light. At this point, the music, still slightly muffled, echoed loudly as if she were outside the doors of a nightclub. As the vibration pounded through her being, she could not help but notice the hanging lightbulb sway slightly back and forth. She stared, perplexed by its movement.

*Creeaaak, thud.*

*What was that?* She wondered. Past the hanging light, the hallway turned to the left. As quietly as a mouse, Pearl stretched her head around the corner and found a door standing before her.

This door appeared matte black and had six panels, three stacked vertically on the left and three on the right. Underneath the door, she noticed flashing lights shining through the crack and the vibration of heavy music pulsing below the soles of her feet. What really caught her eye, though, was the door's knob. The knob looked as if it had been melted, not enough to be dysfunctional, but enough to catch her eye. But what really grabbed her attention were the imprints the knob carried of the previous hands of those who had entered the door before her. She squinted, fearful, yet determined. She grabbed ahold of the melted knob and slowly cracked the door open. For a moment, she paused, looking through the crack. Yet, in a few short seconds, a gust of wind came through the sliver of space, pushing the door open wide. Light flooded her vision and beats blared through her ears.

4

Pearl stood as a silhouette in the center of the door frame as her eyes gazed out before her. This room resembled a large, popular, yet rundown nightclub. Blue and white strobe lights flashed through the building, matching the DJ's beats that bumped through two vibrating four-foot subwoofers in the back of the room. The walls were painted black and were covered with neon signs, different shapes, sizes, and sayings, which reminded Pearl of Spark's from back home. This comforted her for a moment.

She walked through the door and closed it behind her, watching it disappear into thin air in the blink of an eye. Through the clouds of smoke, she saw a group of people, around a hundred, partying like there was no tomorrow. Most people were dancing under the blue and white strobes, while other people were talking, sucking face, and taking drugs. But what interested Pearl the most, was that there were people authentically laughing together. Their laughter seemed so genuine that one would think they were nothing less than happy and having the best time of their lives. *In The Maze? There was no way,* Pearl thought. *Who could possibly find happiness in a place like this?*

The smiling faces grew wider the harder they partied. Some people were doing blow, some were just smoking weed. Some were eating shrooms, while others took ecstasy. Some people did ketamine, even LSD and DMT, yet, just about every person there had a beverage in hand. It quickly became clear that everyone in this door appeared *heavily* under the influence.

Seeing these people sent Pearl for a ride on memory lane. Pearl had partied before, in fact, after her parents died, nearly all she did was party. Substances were the cure to healing her wounds, she believed, and forgetting about your problems was the key to living a happy life. However, when she stepped foot into this door, she fell in disbelief. She had never seen partying like this. The drugs were nothing out of the ordinary, but the amount that these people were consuming was unlike anything she had ever seen before. People were chugging handles, snorting mountains, smoking out their lungs, and consuming twenty times the typical amount. For a moment, she looked at these people as if she were looking deep within herself. It became clear that these people were not genuinely happy.

Again, how could they be in a place like this? It was a facade. This method of numbing oneself brought only a temporary sensation of freedom and ease, yet it was no more effective than slapping on a band-aid. Pearl thought about all the substances she had ingested herself over the years to escape the pain and sorrow, when really, it never left her. Rather, the traumas had sunken deeper within her being, toxifying her from the inside and hiding underneath her sad, cold-hearted, lethal layers.

Pearl continued walking forward passing by several small groups of people. Compared to the other doors she had entered thus far, this door had not one monstrous creature in sight. The room was full of mortals, in fact nobody in this door seemed to be interested, let alone care, that Pearl was there. Most of them seemed to be thoroughly enjoying themselves and focusing on nothing but the moment, despite their poisoned minds.

Pearl walked up to a long, glass bar. Behind the bar stood a man, maybe around forty years old, pouring whiskey into a not-so-small shot glass. He looked up at Pearl.

"Can I get you—say, I've never seen you before. Are you new here?"

"Yes, this is my first time here. My name is Pearl."

The bartender smiled, while handing over the shot of whiskey to another lone woman who sat feebly at the bar.

"Well, Pearl, get comfortable, because this is going to be your favorite door of The Maze." The bartender laughed to himself. "What can I get for you?"

"What is this place?" Pearl asked with curiosity, hopeful for help.

"What does it look like to you?" The bartender responded like she had asked a stupid question.

Pearl looked around awkwardly, then back at the man. "Well, my guess would be a club."

"That's a good guess, Pearl. I'm glad your eyes are working. Now what can I get for ya'?

Her eyebrows crinkled inward. "I'm okay, thanks."

"Come on. You gotta have a drink while you're here," he insisted.

Pearl paused for a moment, thinking to herself. Hesitantly, she replied, "I guess I'll do a margarita, please."

The bartender poured a silver tequila from an unlabeled bottle for about three quarters of the way up the ice-filled, salted rim, bucket glass, followed by a mixer, and a lime garnish. He reached his hand out, handing her the drink.

"Thanks," Pearl replied, reaching out for the margarita.

"Whoa, wait!" The bartender's eyes opened wide as her hand reached out toward his. He pulled the drink away from her. "You still have your bracelet?"

Pearl looked at her wrist. "Yeah, I do. Why? Do you not have yours?" She looked over at his hands. The man brought his hands up toward his face and revealed his naked wrists.

"My bracelet is long gone." He set the margarita back on his side of the bar. He pulled out a pint glass, poured her margarita inside, and then whipped out the bottle of tequila, dumping two more ounces inside. "You'll need this." He handed the drink over to Pearl.

"Oh wow. What do I owe you? Or do I even owe you?"

"It's on me." The man walked away, leaving Pearl alone before she could even say thanks.

Pearl grabbed the glass and took a sip. It was strong, in fact, she could not taste anything except the bittersweet taste of tequila, but she did not mind. After everything she had gone through in The Maze thus far, straight tequila sounded like nothing short of fantastic. She took another swig, then began wandering once again.


5


Pearl sauntered through the room with her glass close to her heart. She scanned the room left to right, keeping to herself as she watched the party unfold. Her head floated underneath the flashing lights as she moved forward. Without warning, the crowd of people grew into a mob. People were stumbling into her, accidentally knocking her in her shoulders, sometimes hard enough that she would spill a few sips of her drink. Discomfort swept over her, so she searched for an out.

She made her way through the crowd, pushing through the sweaty, smelly, dancing bodies, until she stepped out of the mob and caught a breath of semi-fresh air. She found herself standing near a lounge set-up in the corner of the room. There sat two couches, one woman, and a mountain of cocaine on the coffee table before her. Pearl took a breath, then a sip, turning her eyes back to the crowd.

"Hey, you! You got any cash on you?" A woman's voice shouted out.

Pearl glanced over her shoulder for a moment.

"Yeah, you," the voice continued. Pearl's eyes met those of the woman sitting on the couch. She had short, purple hair and white, pale skin. Her brown eyes were glazed over, and she had a single piercing looped around her nose. She wore black sneakers, tight blue jeans, and a black, fluffy sweater that looked two sizes too big. Resting on her lap was a half-empty handle of vodka. She motioned to Pearl to come over to her, smiling.

Pearl walked over to the side of the couch.

"You got any cash?" The woman asked.

"Uh," Pearl hesitated, reaching into her pockets. "No, I don't have anything on me, unfortunately."

"I got a hundred," a voice yelled from behind Pearl, waddling over to the girls. He handed over a Franklin to her and gave her a wink.

"Thanks, Charlie. You want a line?"

"Next time, I got Steph waiting for me on the dance floor. Catch ya later!"

"I'll get ya next time!" The woman yelled back. She glanced back at Pearl as she rolled the bill up tightly like a straw. "Thanks anyway. I don't think I've seen you before. What's your name?"

"Pearl Cassel."

"You a seeker or a prisoner?"

"Uh, I think I'm a—"

The woman grabbed hold of her right hand and noticed her stringy bracelet. She threw her arm back by Pearl's side.

"You're a seeker."

"Everyone's been calling me that and I don't know what it means."

"It means you're seeking for your truth. You still have your bracelet, so you still have a chance." The woman leaned over her thighs and hovered her nose over the mountain of blow. She stuck one side of the bill to her right nostril, placed a finger on her left nostril, then snorted greatly. Pearl watched the powder shoot through her nose and up to her skull. The woman's eyes rolled back into her head. "Sit down with me," she demanded, sniffing back the powder.

Pearl sat down wearily on the edge of the couch. She was nervous, yet the conversation with an actual human felt relieving.

"Do you have a bracelet?" Pearl asked.

The purple-haired woman showed her wrists. No bracelet.

"I'm a prisoner. Have been for a long time." Instead of saying 'a long time,' she elongated the word and said 'a *looong* time.' "Everyone in here is a prisoner." The woman's eyes squinted at Pearl, and her lips smirked as she took another swig from the vodka bottle.

"How do you become a prisoner?" Pearl asked innocently.

"You lose his game. You lose your bracelet, just like he wants you to. Some people lose it before they even make it to their first door of The Maze. Other people, like myself, lose it about halfway through. You're lucky that you still have yours. How many doors have you been through so far?"

"This is my sixth door."

"Your sixth door, huh? You're doing pretty well then. Good for you. I would do anything to find my bracelet again. I saw mine last falling overboard into the ocean, sinking down into depths I could never go to. I

knew then that I would be trapped for eternity in this fucking hell hole."
Her eye twitched, and she took another swig.

Pearl felt sorry for her. She could not fathom the idea of staying here forever, in fact she could not make sense of it. Not even close.

"Are you dead?" Pearl asked nervously, but too curious not to.

She spoke with a low, traumatized tone. "Out there, in the real world, yeah. In here though, never. Though I wish more than anything in the world that I was. A person never leaves this place unless they are strong enough to do so. There's only been a handful of people that have made it to the last door of The Maze. What happens at the end? Do they really make it out? Nobody knows. Other than that, everyone you see here has been a prisoner for longer than we could remember. All because of that damned man." She took another gulp and stared off into the distance.

"Doc?" Pearl asked.

"Yeah, him."

Pearl paused for a moment, taking in everything the woman had said so far. She glanced down toward her bracelet and rubbed the remaining chain links and the single pearl she had between her fingers. She glanced back up toward the woman.

"But, how are we all here? If The Maze is a place in my mind, my own head, how can I see you and all of these other people?"

"None of us really know. It's like we all have been put into a different dimension. We all are clueless, but considering that we are all here together must mean we are in some sort of never-ending portal of consciousness. And no matter how many times we try to kill ourselves, and no matter how we attempt to do it, we never can, nor will we ever be able to. The Maze is an endless time loop, a place where time doesn't exist, and if you become a prisoner, you become a prisoner for eternity."

Pearl's heart sank into her stomach. "But what about our bodies? If you die out in the real world, where do they go?" Pearl asked.

"Hell, if I know. They could still be sitting in his god-awful leather chair strapped up for all I know. Although, that would be unlikely considering how many new seekers have made their way through here. Maybe he dumps our bodies somewhere in the woods where nobody would ever find them. Depending on how long the person is in The Maze, that is. Your body can only go so long without water and food, you know."

*No, I don't know,* Pearl thought to herself sarcastically. She took another sip of her margarita, slurping down the heavy tequila, tangy lime juice, and briny salt. With all this information, she felt encouraged to ask more.

"There's a little boy here. He's following me, and he has been since I got here." Pearl swallowed, choking on her words. "He has hundreds of teeth. Maybe even a thousand, and they lie in rows, like a shark. But they aren't normal teeth, some are baby teeth and others look like fangs. And his eyes... his eyes resemble the eyes of a goat, with rectangular pupils, and darker than any set of eyes I have ever seen."

"I see," the woman responded.

Pearl paused, wondering if her words were even being heard. "I think he's a prisoner here, like you."

"He's not," she disagreed.

Pearl raised an eyebrow at her. "So, you know who I am talking about then?"

"No, I don't. I mean, I have never seen him before. But it sounds like that's your chaser."

"My chaser?"

"Yeah. We all have them. Well, seekers still have them, anyways. For the people that couldn't find their way out, the prisoners, like myself, their chaser prevailed."

"What do you mean prevailed?"

"I mean, they prevailed. They won." She took another large swig, and then prepared for another line from the powdered mountain.

"I thought the purpose of The Maze was to just find your way out?"

She laughed. "Sounds like a dream. Not all of them, but many of the monsters or creatures you see within The Maze are really just projections from the darkest parts of your own mind. But just because they are projections, does not mean that they can't hurt you. You see, they're always there, yet it's your mind that's creating them. I mean, it makes sense. The Maze is a portal to our subconscious mind." She paused, taking another swig of vodka. "And when it comes to chasers—they are kind of like the 'boss level' of a video game. Our number one arch-nemeses. The thickest layer that covers our skin. Every seeker has one. That's why you're called seekers,' because you are constantly seeking an escape from your chaser. And, seeking for your life that you still have out there."

Pearl paused a moment, analyzing everything the woman had revealed thus far. "But in one of the doors, me and another seeker were both running from a monster grizzly bear. How could we both see him if he is a projection from my own mind?"

The woman chuckled, pounding back another swig. "Like I said, *many* of the monsters are projections of your own mind. Not all of them. Some just come with the territory, depending on what door you go through. Luckily, the monsters don't come near this door. The party is too much for them to handle I guess."

Pearl fell perplexed, thinking back on all the doors she had gone through so far. "So, if prisoners can't die here, can seekers? I mean, like *really* die." Pearl asked. "I should have died so many times. I even watched someone with a bracelet die right in front of me, in a way that would be impossible to live through."

"No one can ever really *die* here. Sometimes, seekers cross journeys throughout The Maze, but each person in The Maze is on their own journey. You two could even be learning completely different lessons in the same door. You could learn a lesson about judgment, and they could learn a lesson about grief. But whatever happens in The Maze to you is destined to happen for you to become who you are *meant* to be. So, if you see someone die, they learned what they needed to learn, and are on to the next door. You *want* to die in this place. Living here is the real problem."

Pearl took a sip of her drink and instead of tasting tequila on the tip of her tongue, she heard the straw sucking the last bit of liquid from the bottom of the glass. It was probably best that her cup was empty considering how good she felt in such a horrible place. For a moment, she glanced at all the people partying around her like they had zero worries in the world, then she looked back at the woman.

"Why are so many of you prisoners hanging out in this door?"

"Why wouldn't we? You think if we are stuck in The Maze for time without end, we wouldn't be getting fucked up and partying the whole time? What's really fucked up, is that there are prisoners here that don't even come near this door. Those sick fucks are out there in The Maze enjoying The Maze just how it is. Those people deserve to be there, away from the rest of us." She took another swig. "The best part about not dying though, I will admit, is that there is no such thing as getting *too* fucked up. Why wouldn't we party? Wouldn't you if you forever lived in hell?"

The woman had a point. Yet, in that moment, Pearl realized something she never recognized before. As she listened to the woman, she understood that no matter how much they intoxicated their mind, one thing became certain. It never changed the fact that they were still in The Maze, forever suffering in agony, never facing their problems, nor letting them go. They held onto their traumas and buried them deep down inside, continuously intoxicating themselves into oblivion. As insightful the woman was, Pearl could not help but feel her pain. Pearl looked back at her as if she were looking in a mirror. She knew there was no way she could stay in The Maze. She was determined to find her way out.

The woman leaned over, put the bill to her nose, and inhaled the powder. "Ahhh, that's nice. You want some?"

"I'm fine, thanks though." Pearl denied, yet flashed her a small smile. "And thank you for answering all my questions, too."

The woman smiled back. "Of course. I know what it's like to be a newbie in this place. It's fucked up. The Maze is a twisted, horrific, gut-wrenching place to be in. Whether it's here, running through the doors in this other-worldly dimension, or in the real world, where our darkest thoughts consume our lives. The mind can be a scary fucking place."

Pearl kept her smile and nodded. She got up from her seat and stuck out her hand to shake the woman's. "Thank you. You have helped me so much."

The woman stood up onto her feet and wrapped her arms around Pearl. "Stay strong, friend."

6

Pearl found herself wandering through the party alone. She had returned her empty glass back to the bar, politely denied a second drink, then explored the room some more. In one corner, she noticed a group of men gambling over a game of cards. In another, she witnessed a small orgy between two men and three women. Nobody seemed to mind, in fact, Pearl realized that orgies here were quite normal when she passed another one only ten feet up ahead. *At least they had some sort of pleasure to look forward to,* Pearl thought. *Good for them.* She kept to herself, stayed low, and continued ambling forward.

Suddenly, a random arm flung over Pearl's shoulder. "Hey!" A young man greeted her.

"Hello." Pearl felt immediately uncomfortable. She looked down at his wrists and noticed no bracelet.

The man pulled her closer to him and yelled in her ear through the beats of the music. "So, you're the newbie, aye?"

Pearl did not say a word.

"Hey guys! We have a seeker over here!" The man yelled out to a couple of other guys from afar. The other men stampeded over to them, laughing and cheering like a pack of wild animals.

The man pulled Pearl over to a blue round sofa with a round, wooden coffee table off to the side, while the obnoxious men followed closely behind. He sat her down with him, sitting less than an inch from her. Pearl's breath became short and the hair on her arm rose tall toward the flashing strobe lights.

"Yo, Paul! You got the shit?" He asked one of the others.

"Fuck yeah," he roared back. The man pulled a backpack from his shoulders. He unzipped the bag, flipped it upside down over the table, and emptied everything from inside. The bag released plastic baggies full of substances, syringe needles, spoons, hundred-dollar bills, and more. The men shuffled the baggies all over the table, picking their poison for their individual pleasure. Except for Pearl, they all laughed with casual intoxication. Meanwhile, their group began to attract a crowd. People from all parts of the room began to make their way toward their table. People stopped their dancing, left their seats from the bar, and even the people in the orgies came over after they finished. Pearl sat unnervingly, scanning the eyes of all those who stared back.

"Which one do you want to do?" The man asked her.

Pearl looked back down toward the table, then back at the man. "I'm fine, thank you."

The man's chuckle morphed into a giant belly laugh. His friends copied him, and so did some people in the crowd.

"That's not how this works," he replied. "You see, if you are here with us, you got to pick your poison. What will it be?"

Pearl's stomach turned even more. She looked at the man, looked back down toward the substances, and then up toward the crowd. Many people began cheering, and some began to shout out things like, "Do it!" "Let's get on with it, already!" "Let's see what you got!" Between the chanting and the shuffling bodies, Pearl noticed the girl with the purple hair standing from afar, watching Pearl through the swarm of prisoners. Her eyes stared at Pearl, wide with concern. However, she nodded at Pearl, reassuring her that everything would be okay.

Pearl looked back at the man. "What are they?" She asked.

"You have to try to find out!" A smile crept across his face.

Pearl did not want to do it. Not one part of her had a desire to ingest this poison into her body. Yet, she knew she had no other choice, and for her to move forward, she understood what she needed to do. Pearl scanned the baggies one by one, debating on which one to choose. They all looked the same. Inside the plastic bags, she noticed a white powder, some more or less than others. Unclear as to what she was getting herself into, she closed her eyes tight, reached her hand out on the table, and randomly picked a bag. She held it in her fist, opened her eyes, and glanced down at her prize. She chose one of the smallest baggies with only a small amount of dust inside. The crowd grew more excited, chanting at the top of their lungs.

"Pick another one," the man sitting by her side said.

She looked at him confused. She grabbed her first baggy and returned it back to the table.

"No!" He stopped her. "I mean, grab another one, along with that one."

Pearl stared at him like he was crazy. Maybe he was, but he probably did not care. Pearl slowly set the small baggy back onto her lap. Again, she closed her eyes, hovered her hand over the table, and then randomly reached down like a claw machine. She opened her eyes and revealed her winnings. This time, she chose a big plastic baggy, with a lot more powder than the first. She set it on her lap and looked back at the man.

"One more." He smiled deviously. The crowd kept wild. Pearl gulped, closed her eyes, and shuffled her hand through the baggies. She grabbed one more, brought it close toward her lap, and opened her eyes. Another small plastic baggy.

"Good, good," the man said. He took the bags out of her hands and cleared a space on the table. He unzipped each bag, shook out some powder, and created three lines. He picked up a hundred, rolled it up tight, and passed it to her. Every prisoner gawked toward Pearl, waiting for her next move.

She stared at the man with intense worry in her eyes. Her head softly shook side to side as she stared down at the drugs before her. For a moment, she flashed a glance to the woman with the nose piercing. She had disappeared.

Pearl looked down at the lines once again.

"I can't do it," Pearl admitted.

The man by her side let out a loud, repulsive laugh. The crowd followed him. Yet, within a split second, his laughter subsided, and his eyes glared deeply into Pearl's. "We all had to do it, now it's your turn."

Pearl remained frozen, her shoulders rising toward her ears and her jaw clenched with fear.

"If you don't," the man continued, as he pulled out a sharp, jagged knife from his coat pocket, "I'll slit every part of your body into tiny little pieces, including that bracelet from your wrist. The choice is yours."

Pearl looked him in the eyes with sadness. She put the paper to her nose, hovered over the powder, and sniffed the first line. A sensation of exhilarating euphoria overflowed her mind and body. Her pupils dilated and she felt her heart pound just about out of her chest. She felt invincible, like she stood on top of the world. *Cocaine,* she thought. Pearl had tried it a few times before, but as she grew older, she hadn't cared for it much. But, at that moment, it felt nice to release her worries.

"Woohoo! Woohoo!" The prisoners went wild, shouting out loud and hollering with joy. Many knocked their glasses together and opened their gullets, while others snorted lines themselves.

"Keep going," the man demanded.

Pearl looked at him, then back at powder below her. *Two left,* she thought to herself. She put the bill to her nose, hung over the second line, and snorted. Within another few seconds, she instantly became light-headed. Her vision became unclear, and her mind and body flooded with a feeling of uncomfortable numbness. She could feel her heart begin to slow, then speed up, then almost stop. Pearl grew dizzier, as she looked around at the mob of prisoners cheering her on. As much as she tried to focus, she could not tell what she was looking at, and the feeling of this drug hit so intensely that the voices of the chanting crowd began to grow muffled. From immediately going up, she felt herself drop like a bag of bricks. She was not sure as to what drug this was, but it felt like a downer. Whatever it is, she did not like it. A tear rolled down her cheek, yet she could not even feel it. Pearl began swaying back and forth in her seat, trying her best to sit up straight. Yet, the combination of drugs and alcohol became so intense that she fell back into the sofa, sinking deep into the comforter. The crowd shouted louder with their fists in the air.

"Last one," the man whispered into Pearl's ear while the crowd chanted "Last one! Last one! Last one!"

The man pushed Pearl's back off the couch, helped lean her over the table, and pulled her hair to the side. Pearl hovered over the last line, swaying in her seat, while shaking the hundred at the edge of her right nostril. She paused for a moment, trying her best to take in one last breath. Until suddenly, she sniffed the last line, inhaling almost all of it. An incredible feeling of painful shock struck through her. In a second, she felt a piercing sensation stab through the front of her skull, and her nose began dripping blood. Her eyes rolled into the back of her head, and both her mind and her body lost control. The crowd began fading right before her eyes and everything around her started to spin. Her body began to convulse, and within a single breath, her head came down like a hammer and slammed on top of the table. Her whole world went black.

# Door #7
# I Am Crazy

1

Life struck through her being once again, shocking her from the inside out. Like an overdose shot with adrenaline, her eyes exploded open, her back shot up and off The Maze floor, and her breath struck back into her lungs. She gasped for a few breaths, just like the times before.

As her thoughts became clear, she instantly glanced down at her wrist and began counting the chain links. Only four remained hanging. A smile peaked along her face, for a moment, as she let out a sigh of hope and release. *I am going to make it, I am going to survive,* she thought to herself. As she sat with this relief, and with her next breath, she became overwhelmed with her next ego death of The Maze.

A sensation swept over her; a feeling that was so intense it felt almost unbearable. For the first time, Pearl felt the numbness she had coated over her mind and body slowly lift up and off of her being. For years, she had been suppressing her emotions by shoving them down, deep inside, hiding them underneath excessive toxins that she consumed almost daily. Alcohol, drugs, they all loaded the gaping hole within her heart, filling the void with a temporary, artificial sensation of release. This constant escape she yearned for was nothing more than disguise, and the more she shoved down her shadows, the more they grew over time, further stacking layers on top of layers over her highest Self. In that moment, her heavy, hidden emotions that she had buried deep within rose to the surface, flooding her being with emotions of sadness, anger, frustration, and grief. Despite her new perception of the present moment she gained in the door before, as her shadows began to surface, her monkey mind began running wild with thoughts, thoughts like "I am miserable," "I am crazy," "I am this," and "I am that." Constantly smacking labels on top of herself like a bandaid on a wound. It became clear to her that suppressing her problems, running away from her problems, and intoxicating her mind to escape her problems, would never allow her wounds to truly ever heal. Now that she uncovered her shadows, to move forward, she knew she would be forced to face, feel, and free the emotions she had clung tightly onto for all these years. By releasing her poisoned mind, she granted her emotions permission to be felt. She was ready to feel the festering feelings. She was ready to let them go. A feeling of empowerment flowed through her so intensely that a grateful tear trickled down her cheek. She smiled, chuckling to herself with a sigh of relief.

Pearl pushed herself up and off the cold, red floor, took a conscious deep breath in and out, and began down the path to uncertainty once again.

2

The blood red hallway stretched long out in front of her. At the end of the path, she noticed the hall break off into three different directions, each leading to their own pit of darkness. She swallowed a dry lump down her throat, gritted her teeth underneath lips, then crept ahead.

Her body moved forward, stepping one foot after another. Pearl patrolled onward with prudence. As she made her way toward the diverging halls, she peaked her head down each hall, squinting her eyes to focus on anything she could possibly see before her. However, with limited light in each hall, the only thing Pearl could perceive was darkness stretching out before her. She stopped for a moment, tapping into her intuition to feel which direction called to her more. Something inside of her felt drawn to the hallway on the right, more so than the other two. So, Pearl instinctively walked to the right, making her way down the hallway.

Pearl walked for about twenty minutes, agilely following the zigzagged hallway with her hands against the wall. Suddenly, as she made her way further down the hall, a loud, horrific bang from behind her echoed and vibrated the path. Immediately following, a random light that hung in the middle of the hall shot on, illuminating the uncharted territory. Pearl rapidly turned her body around to see where the loud crash came from. When she did, she noticed the pathway behind her became closed off, with a dead end near. The rhythm of Pearl's heart picked up and danced underneath her chest while sweat trickled down the sides of her face. Yet, she remained strong. She took another conscious, deep breath in through her nose, and a great exhale out of her mouth. Turning back was no longer an option. She had no choice but to move forward.

Pearl turned her body back toward her original route, only this time, with a dangly lightbulb lighting the path ahead. As she continued forward, around the corner stood a large, double door with two small windows, lonesome, at the end of the hall.

She skulked up to the double door, peeking her eyes through the window to see what it could be. She noticed a long, lit-up hallway that stretched for what seemed to be an endless distance. The floor was made of grey, rubber sheet flooring, and the walls were painted off-white. Scattered throughout the hall sat random medical equipment like IV stands, sanitation stations, vital monitors, syringes, and scalpels. There was a person hunched over in a medical gown, with their arm wrapped over the neck of a nurse for physical support, staggering through the hall. A little further, she could barely make out the figure of a man talking to another man, one of which had a white coat and stethoscope hanging from his body. Without thinking twice, Pearl pushed the doors open wide in front of her. They hurled out and away from her body, as if she were welcomed in with open arms. Pearl had entered the seventh door with little to no hesitation.

Pearl engulfed herself with her new surroundings. Once in, she looked over her shoulder for a moment, and found herself staring at a white wall with a single chair sitting against it. The double doors vanished. Pearl turned her head back forward and began making her way through the hospital-like hallway. Down the hall, she passed multiple different people. She noticed a few creatures; some had fur, some were skinless, some had fangs, and some had dislocated jaws hanging heavy with no teeth at all. She looked away, not wanting any part of them. As she walked past these creatures of the dark, she made her way past a few mortals with naked wrists. *Prisoners,* she thought to herself. However, the mortal prisoners she noticed appeared unharmed and unphased. They walked quickly past, their faces expressionless, and their eyes in a daze. Physically, their bodies appeared in decent condition, yet something about their blank, emotionless faces and lack of presence made Pearl feel uncomfortable in her own skin. They seemed to be out of their minds; mentally checked out.

As she crept through the eerie halls, a woman with a nursing uniform suddenly emerged from one of the sliding glass doors along one of the barren walls, aggressively grabbing Pearl by the arm.

"No, no, no, honey. You are supposed to go this way!" She exclaimed as she pulled Pearl toward another door off to the side. The woman opened a random door for Pearl and vigorously pushed her in, closing the door behind her.

Pearl stumbled inside. She looked around herself and noticed that this room she had entered was in fact the same, exact hospital that she attended to every Friday morning. In front of her stood an identical stair-well leading up to the second floor of the building, the same staircase she walked up weekly. Without thinking, she walked forward, naturally gravitated up the stairs, and followed the familiar path. When she reached the top, she continued down the hall, just as she did in the real world.

She wandered gradually forward, holding her body close to her core, and clenching every muscle she had. As she walked further, she squinted her eyes at a sign hovering over a door that read "Psychiatry, Waiting Room One." She stopped for a moment and she stood up tall, lifting her chin slightly up toward the sky, puffing her chest out in front of her, and rolling her shoulders back and down her spine. Pearl took one more conscious breath in through her nose, and a conscious breath out of her mouth. She walked ahead, pulled the heavy door open wide, and waddled inside.

The door swung open toward her body, presenting her with the same layout as the waiting room she waited anxiously in every week. However, in this waiting room, strange, yet familiar faces that she had seen a few weeks prior patiently waited for her once again.

First, she recognized the same old man that sat zoned out in the real world. Yet, in this dimension, he appeared different. His glasses were pushed up on the top of the bridge of his nose, and his skin was tighter than she remembered. His cheeks seemed flusher than before, and his eyebrows were full. He wore the same outfit she saw him in last; a brown fedora and a loose, cotton sweater vest with big, black buttons. Rather than the man sitting slouched over with his jaw dropped in a daze, this old man sat straight up tall, with a wide, uncomfortable smile stretching from ear to ear.

The next person she noticed was the woman in her late thirties. She looked just about identical to the first woman she had remembered; she had brown hair tied in a bun, and her deep, dark eyelashes were still longer than ever. Her olive brown skin appeared greyer than before, yet she appeared to be much calmer than what Pearl recalled. She, too, had a creepily long smile plastered on her face.

After, Pearl recognized the young man, Daniel, who sat alone in the middle of the room, in a television trance. Pearl reminisced, for a moment, about the boy laughing to himself and the screen, easily amused and full of energy in the real world. However, the boy sat silent in this world, not moving a single muscle. His mouth appeared to be stitched shut all the way across.

Lastly, she noticed the mother and son from that same day, waiting amongst the rest of them. The woman had the same long, blonde hair braided down her back, and her skin hugged her insides tighter than before. Her demeanor seemed satisfied and happy, as she also had a great, big smile painted on her face. Sitting by her side was her four or five-year-old son with shaggy, blonde hair. He, too, sat with an awkward smile. Despite the subtle differences she had of her memories, she noticed that all five of these familiar faces had one thing in common: their eyes were flooded with pools of obscure, horrific darkness. Nothing but black swarmed their sockets. This frightened her, yet not nearly as much as the presence of one, familiar face.

In the very back corner of the room, she recognized a face that made her skin crawl up her limbs and down her back. The boy, with a thousand teeth, sat alone, smiling at Pearl with his wicked smile and piercing, demonic eyes. Pearl's wide eyes met his, and she gasped for a breath as she held onto her exhale. The muscles in Pearl's face quickly grew stiff. In that instant, she felt completely paralyzed. Her stomach crawled up her throat.

Suddenly, a woman's voice spoke aloud. "I can help you, dear."

Pearl turned toward the receptionist. Like the real world, the receptionist had short, brown, curly hair and brown, rectangular, prescription glasses resting on the bridge of her nose. Yet, behind her lenses, her eyes were deluged with black like the others. Her eyebrows furrowed, and the corners of her mouth curled up toward her temples. Underneath her eyes, streamed bloody tears down her lifeless, white skin. Pearl felt absolutely petrified.

The receptionist's smile crept across her face. "Hello sweetie, we have been waiting for you."

"For—for me?" Pearl stuttered back.

"Yes, dear. Let me just get you checked in," the receptionist responded, typing away on her rundown keyboard. As she did, Pearl slowly looked behind her at the boy with a thousand teeth. However, when she did, she saw he was gone. Yet, the sensation of fear still dictated her entire being. Her eyes squinted as she quickly scanned the room.

The receptionist cleared her throat, grabbing Pearl's attention. "They are ready for you." She said, gritting her teeth at Pearl.

The doors on the other side of the room flung open toward Pearl, with a long, beat-up stretcher rushing through. Behind the stretcher ran three creatures, pushing it from behind at full force.

Two of the creatures had the body of a human, running on two legs and pushing the bed with two arms, carried by nothing more than skin and bones. Their bodies appeared pale, almost snow white. They looked weak and had little to no meat on their bones. Even the muscles in their faces appeared nonexistent, their cheeks sunken into pits and their bones jutting out below their unholy, crazed, black eyes.

The third creature running by their side had an egg-shaped, bald, white head with veins protruding all over. He had holes where his ears would be, and a long, pointy chin. Like a reptile, he had thin, muted, pallid scales covering his whole body. He had another two holes in the center of his face where his nose would be, and his pin-sized pupils rested within his sunken sockets. The creature's mouth dropped open wide with a smile, his tongue drooping with thick drool dripping down. He appeared to be almost alien-like, and he walked with a hunch, his pelvis lifted and his tailbone tucked in. The three of them ran fast on their toes.

Pearl turned her body toward the oncoming stretcher and jolted back. The creature with pinned eyes ran around the stretcher, grabbed both of Pearl's biceps and yanked her down onto the bed. Her back flopped down onto the stretcher with force, while the other creatures helped keep her down. They grabbed ahold of her hands and pulled them straight down by her sides, with her palms facing down. They reached for the rope and tied her wrists tightly to the stretcher, followed by her ankles. In that instant, she had become immobile, and her body fell into the hands of evil.

Pearl's head wavered back and forth in terror as she screamed at the top of her lungs. "Let me go! Please, stop! Please! What the fuck do you want with me!?"

The creature with the pinned eyes and hanging jaw hovered over her, looking down at her with his unrighteous, wicked smile. The creature did not speak. Instead, he lifted his hand up and placed it on her face. He dragged his nails down her cheek with ease, leaving behind light, red scratch marks. He continued to smile at her, as if everything was going to be okay.

"Please," she whispered, her lips quivering.

The being shook his head back and forth at her. He dragged his finger back up the side of her face, grabbed hold of another piece of rope, and tied her head down like the rest of her. Suddenly, her vision focused on nothing but the ceiling above. Just like that, the patient had fallen under their control.

4

The three immortals pulled the door open and shoved her through. They ran down the hall with her, pushing the stretcher with excitement and pleasure like kids running to get in line for a ride at a carnival. Pearl observed the ceiling above her, passing can light after can light hanging from the bare, white ceiling. Suddenly, as the creatures rammed her further down the hall, the ceiling began to shift shape and color. From the white walls and bright lights, the ceiling morphed into blood red, cement walls, illuminated by only a few flickering lightbulbs swaying side to side overhead. The creatures pushing her grew louder with laughter, laughing so intensely like they could not be more excited for what was to come. Pearl closed her eyes, clenched her jaw, and breathed short, shallow breaths in and out of her nose.

The four of them quickly approached an operating room around the corner. They rolled Pearl inside, placing her in the center of the room. The room appeared small, cluttered, and congested with medical equipment. Electrical wires hung along the walls, syringes lied on dirty countertops, surgical instruments were scattered all over, and crusted blood appeared splattered on the walls and floors from previous patients. The room flickered from one, dim lightbulb hanging in the center, and it exposed the off-grey, tattered walls that looked as if they were falling at the seams.

The creatures released their grips, turned their backs, and scavenged the room for supplies.

"What do we have here?" One of the creatures asked aloud.

"We have an extremely sick patient. She needs immediate surgery," another immortal responded.

"I'm not sick," Pearl defended.

Pin eyes turned toward Pearl, slithering his lips closer to her ear, and whispered. "You're in the hands of professionals, baby. We know just how to take care of you."

Pearl jolted her body and clenched her fists with rage. "Get the fuck away from me."

All three creatures paused like time froze over. They shifted their attention toward Pearl, then toward one another. One of the black-eyed, meatless creatures replied in an unfamiliar language, while the other two listened. Each of them spoke in the same, peculiar tongue, one that Pearl had never heard before, leaving her clueless. Finally, the black-eyed creatures dispersed, fiddling with medical equipment, while the short, pin-eyed creature slithered over to the side of the stretcher and looked down at Pearl with a wicked smile.

"You're so confident for such a sick, helpless human," he commented.

Pearl's eyes pierced back into his. She grit her teeth harder and her blood boiled underneath her skin. "I'm not sick." She repeated more firmly, trying to convince him otherwise, yet no matter how hard she tried, it did not matter. The real person she needed to convince was herself.

Every day, in the real world, she believed herself to be mentally sick. When she went to see her therapist, she felt crazy, out of her mind, and unworthy to live. She believed she was a freak for going to therapy, and she believed living a depressed life was simply part of her nature. She convinced herself so much that she allowed these emotions to pollute her mind, and ultimately, her reality, permitting rotten layers to grow over her even more.

"What makes a person so confident in a place like this? The Maze? You must have been sicker than we thought. You'll never escape this place. You'll be trapped here with the rest of us. Forever suffering like you did out there in the real world. What difference does it make?" He continued, pacing beside her with his hands behind his back.

"You aren't real," Pearl whispered quietly out loud.

"What did you say?"

"You. Are. Not. Real."

The creature laughed out loud. "I'm not real, you say? Who is to say what is real or not? What makes something real versus not being real?"

"You are a projection. You're not a prisoner, you're a monster. A monster of my own mind."

"What makes something real and what doesn't, Pearl?" The creature asked again, as he slowly turned toward one of the other monsters in the room. "Salackeen tonu manelor sen!"

The creature nodded, rushed over to one of the filth-covered countertops, and scavenged for a syringe. He picked up a needle the size of a pencil and raced it back over to the monster. The monster nodded back, dismissing him once again.

"I think if you can feel it, then it is real. Don't you?" He asked Pearl, flicking the needle over her head.

"Get the fuck away from me."

"Such harsh language for such an innocent girl. I just want to know if I am real. If *this* is real just like you said ever so confidently. I am curious if you can feel this." The pin-eyed creature stabbed the syringe into Pearl's right arm. The needle pierced deep into her vein, injecting her with a black fluid that flooded throughout her blood, her body, and finally, her mind. The injection felt nothing less that pure torture, misery, and anguish. Her entire body felt like it was being stung by a thousand box jellyfish. The pain felt so excruciating, Pearl could not help but scream out loud as her body seized. The creature smiled sinisterly and asked, "Can you feel this?"

Pearl's body jolted as hard as it could while being tied down. "Wha— What are yo—you doing to me? What is th—this," Pearl stuttered, her lips quaking and drooling uncontrollably. Within a few seconds, black stars began to make shape in Pearl's vision. The room began spinning slowly, as if time were coming to a halt. Suddenly, her screams grew silent. Pearl's eyes rolled into the back of her head, and in an instant, her vision grew completely obscured. Her body convulsed with terror and adrenaline overflowed throughout her entire being. Her heart beat out of her chest and her body soaked in sweat. Yet, despite her tranquilized vision, Pearl remained conscious, and could still hear everything going on around her.

"She is heavily sedated, doctor. What shall we do next?" One of the monsters spoke.

Pearl, with all her power, tried to yell "No, no n— no," out loud. Unfortunately, with drugs injected into her veins, she was incapable of speaking clearly. Her lips were so numb that they could barely even move. Pearl grew debilitated, paralyzed, and powerless.

"I think it is time for surgery. Send in the surgeon." Another voice spoke.

Pearl cried and slurred aloud some more. Suddenly, she heard a door opening wide in the room. Incoming was the sound of feet stepping toward the bed where she lied defenselessly. The sound of more footsteps scurried on in after.

"Hello Doctor." "It's time, Doctor." "She's ready for surgery, Doctor."

"Don't do this," Pearl tried to say, yet she sounded so fucked up on whatever it was they shot inside her, that they could hardly make any sense of the words leaving her numbed lips.

"What is wrong with this one?"

"Nothing out of the ordinary. Another mentally ill patient lost in The Maze of their mind."

Her body jolted slightly, her breath grew rapid, and her heart pulsed inconsistently. Then, amidst the chaos, a cold, chilling hand laid across Pearl's forehead, and an outsider voice whispered into her ear. "Do not worry, young girl. We are going to take your pain away." The voice faded, leaving behind the soft sounds of laughter.

Suddenly, the sound of a medical saw echoed throughout the room. With all her might, Pearl tried her hardest to open her heavily influenced eyes, yet the drugs were so intense that her eyes rolled deeper back into her skull. The sound of the saw spun closer and closer toward her ear, ringing her eardrum deafeningly to the point she believed they were about to bleed. Pearl's body laid lifeless on the stretcher, while each limb vibrated numb. It was not until Pearl's last breath, the razor-sharp saw sliced through her right temple, ripping through her flesh, and opening her skull. Pearl's jaw dropped open wide, and without thinking she released a passionate scream. Within that moment of pain and suffering, her consciousness turned off, and the world around her fell silent. She barely felt a thing.

# Door #8
# I Am a Slave to my Thoughts

1

Life flashed right before Pearl's eyes. She gasped for a dramatic breath in, sucking air into her lungs like a balloon about to pop. Her back shot up from the concrete floor and her eyes busted open. Instantly, she rubbed her temples, trying to find any evidence of the traumatizing torcher she had experienced before. Yet, not even a single scratch. She sat winded, taking a moment to recollect her breath and her thoughts once again. As she did so, she made sense of her surroundings. She had returned to The Maze, feeling lighter than she did before. As her breath slowly began to flow smooth and steady, a part of her felt as if something was missing. At first, she could not tell. She knew it felt light, like a weight lifted off her shoulders. She felt good, maybe even great, despite all that she had gone through thus far. That is when it hit her; the seventh lesson of The Maze.

For years of Pearl's young life, she assumed her depression to be a sickness, and she convinced herself that she had to be downright insane. Rather than looking at these feelings as separate, she simply believed them to be part of her. If she felt sad, she would believe sadness was the only way to feel. If she felt like she was crazy for going to therapy every week, she truly believed herself to be out of her mind. *What is wrong with me? How can I be happy when I don't even know what happiness is?* She would constantly wonder, brainwashing her mind even further. By attaching to her emotions and her crucifying, judgmental thoughts, Pearl subconsciously manifested her own, disturbing reality. Yet, how she felt on the inside did not equal to who she truly was. Pearl felt crazy, yet that did not mean she *was* crazy. She felt depressed, yet that did not mean she, her soul within, was depressed. These feelings of sadness, anger, and out of one's mind were just that, *a feeling*. They were temporary, and rather than attaching to them and labeling them as part of her being, they simply required recognition, acknowledgment, a moment to feel, and a moment to let go. For the first time in her life, she realized that she was not her sickness, her depression, nor was she crazy for feeling a certain way. She recognized this layer as an extra load on her back that did nothing but hurt her, tear her down, and weaken her, physically, mentally, and spiritually. With a conscious breath in, she removed the layer and she let the weight from her shoulders go. This realization made her smile. While accepting her emotions to not be a part of her, little did she know that detaching from her thoughts would not be that easy.

She blinked her glazed eyes from the tranquil sensation running through her body. As she returned her attention back to the present moment, she immediately shifted her gaze down to her wrist and admired the one less link. Only three chain links remained along with the shiny, pink pearl. Pearl took a mighty breath in through her nose, and a richer exhale that poured from her mouth. She sat on the floor, smiling wide as a single tear of gratitude rolled down her cheek. She chuckled to herself, finding amusement from all that she had learned. Her heart grew warm with that moment of presence. Suddenly, the walls of The Maze began to shake the stretched, dim hallway. Pearl swallowed a dry gulp, pushed herself up to standing, and set foot back onto her journey down The Maze once again.

2

Pearl walked with speed down the cold, blood red hallway. Anticipation swept over her body, adrenaline rushed through her veins, and her blood boiled underneath her chilled skin. As she sauntered further into the unknown, her nostrils began to burn from the familiar, rotting stench that lingered through The Maze. However, compared to the halls before, the smell of scum grew so overwhelming within this hall that she could practically taste it on the tip of her tongue. Pearl covered her mouth and walked faster into the abyss.

More time passed, until the walls around her began to tremble even more. Particles of dust began to stir and fall off the walls, floating down toward Pearl and the cold, concrete floor. She looked up with concern as the walls shook even harder. Pearl picked up her steadily moving feet and went about running, as if the building were about to collapse.

Pearl ran faster than her mind could think. She knew her destination would be near, so she kept onward, facing every obstacle The Maze had to throw at her.

Finally, after running for what felt like forever, the end of the hall grew near. At the end, Pearl could see a door. This door looked like an ordinary door that one would see in a home. It was made of wood and painted plain white, outlined with a white, wooden frame, and an average, brass doorknob. The rhythm of Pearl's heart began to pound. Her eyes stared deeply at the doorknob as she awaited her next move.

Out of nowhere, a cracking sound began to split through the hallway. Pearl shot a glance in all different directions. Before her eyes, she could see the cement wall splitting in two, cracking from the wall directly next to her right, traveling quickly up toward the endless ceiling. *Earthquake,* she thought to herself. *Or another part of the game.* She considered both without wasting time. Pearl followed the cracking of the cement until it split up into the darkness. That moment, a loud crash echoed from the back end of the hallway, and the ceiling quickly became clear. At the other end of the hall, the ceiling began crashing down, crumbling closer and closer to Pearl. As if a catastrophic earthquake began shaking the walls around her, the ceiling began collapsing so quickly that without another thought, she flipped her body around, gripped the brass doorknob, and shoved the door open. With her eyes closed tight, Pearl ran inside, slamming the bare door closed behind her. The quaking became still. Alas, she had entered the eighth door of The Maze.

3

Pearl slowly peeled her eyes open. Through this door, she found herself inside of what looked like an old, rural cabin. It had four walls poorly constructed of logs, as if someone had just chopped down some trees and stacked them unevenly on top of one another. There were two pictures framed up along the wall, and they each had a drawing of what appeared to be a window frame with a sunny, blue sky and a lush field of grass underneath. Besides those two drawings, there were no real windows. In one corner sat a fake, plastic plant, and by its side sat a single, lit lantern on top of an old-fashioned, wooden desk. In another corner of the room rested a ragged rocking chair with a maroon-colored comforter, and to its right stood a fireplace with a small fire burning within. Pearl noticed another door, locked, and a staircase leading up to a second story with little to no light. She immediately felt uneasy.

Pearl turned back around toward the door she had entered to see if it would disappear like the rest. It vanished, of course, leaving Pearl to face the next layer of her very own mind.

Pearl slowly turned her body back around, scanning the unnerving cabin once again. She took a step forward, creaking the floor below her, making her way further inside. She observed her surroundings, absorbing every detail. Suddenly, up above, the sound of footsteps creaked their way across the ceiling. Fear crept through Pearl's body once again. She stopped for a moment, looked around in every direction, then ran toward an empty corner. She remained still, her breath short, and her heartbeat rapid.

The footsteps slowly began to make their way down the staircase. From the second story came a woman wearing a long, blue nightgown with knitted, grey socks. She had long, brown hair that fell past her bottom, wrinkled skin, and crystal blue eyes that twinkled, despite the low light. However, she wore a deep frown along her face and appeared to be more than upset. She looked throughout the room, until she locked eyes on Pearl.

"You! Where the fuck have you been? The toilet isn't going to clean itself." She staggered over to Pearl, grabbing her by the arm. "And you're out of uniform. You want to tell me why?"

Pearl stared at her blankly, coming up with something to say back. "I—I don't know. I was feeling uncomfortable?" Not her best line, but the best she could come up with in the heat of the moment.

"Uncomfortable? You think I give a fuck about your comfort? Get a move on." The woman yelled, yanking Pearl from the corner and pushing her ahead, forcing her toward the stairs.

Pearl faltered up the stairs, step by step, taking her sweet time. As she made her way closer toward the top, her eyes caught glance of her new surroundings through the stair's railing. Through the bars, she noticed a room, slightly furnished with an old rocking chair, a ragged coffee table, a hutch, and a tall, flickering, floor lamp. Across the room stood an entry to another hall, with a few doors standing between.

"Can you move your feet any faster?" The enraged woman asked, shoving Pearl further up the stairs. She began skipping every other step, until she finally reached the top. "Follow me," demanded the woman.

Pearl followed. The woman led Pearl through the room and toward the other hall, bringing her face to face with one of the doors.

"Here you go." The woman twisted the knob, pulled the door open, and shoved Pearl inside, forcing her into one of the most horrid bathrooms she had ever walked into. The room wafted with a rotten smell so vile that she could barely breathe without gagging. Just like in the hall of The Maze, she could just about taste it. It reeked more than rank.

"What the fuck do you want me to do in here?" Pearl asked defensively. The woman responded with wide, surprised eyes, wondering if Pearl were serious. Then, she let out a big, obnoxious laugh. She walked up to Pearl, opened her hand wide, and slapped her across the face, *hard*.

"Don't you ever speak to me that way again, you hear me? You are in my house, so you play by my rules. You best not be forgetting your place here. You are the slave, and I am your master. Now clean, you worthless piece of shit." The woman reached into a hall closet, pulled out a soggy, old sponge caked with mildew, old food, and mold, a mop, a stained rag, and a few cleaning products. She threw them into the bathroom with Pearl and slammed the door shut.

Pearl held her breath, for a moment, as she rubbed the side of her slapped face. Her skin burned with the slightest touch. She looked at the mirror and examined the palm mark grow more red. As she gazed at her tortured reflection, she took an involuntary breath in, inhaling the disgusting shit smell through her mouth until it gagged her. She covered her mouth and nose, barely breathing, and peered all around her.

The bathroom was small, and it appeared to be stained with grime as though it hadn't been cleaned in a century. The floor had pee marks and shit stains all over. The sink had maggots crawling out from the drain, and there were thick, white spider webs covering every single corner of the room. Pearl could not even imagine what was hiding underneath the toilet lid. She could barely get herself to get near it, let alone touch it. She stared from the other side of the bathroom, about four feet away, with disturbed eyes and a swirling stomach. With the next whiff, she hurled in her mouth.

Pearl plugged her nose. She closed her eyes, lifted her chin slightly, and swallowed the bile that slithered up her throat. Her eyes began to water, seeping at the lids and dripping down her cheeks. She looked down at the toilet and took a few steps forward until the stench gagged her again, so much so that she had no choice but to vomit into the infested sink by her side. After she purged, she wiped the saliva from her bottom lip, held her breath, then glared back at the toilet. As she reached for the lid—

*WHAM!* A crash echoed outside of the room, followed by a disturbed wail. Pearl turned her head and pressed her ear into the door, listening closely to the other side.

"What are you doing to me? What are you—"

WHACK. The voice halted as the sound of a body being beaten sounded through the cabin. Pearl gasped, covering her mouth once again. She backed away from the door, staring with distress. The screams of terror vibrated the floor below her feet as the torture continued. After one more beating, the cries subsided, and the hall had suddenly fallen quiet.

Pearl's breath flowed short. She stood, paralyzed with fear, staring at the door with only her imagination to paint a picture of the agony that stood on the other side. She lowered her hands from her mouth, discon-necting from her sense of smell as much as she could. She took a few steps and reached for the knob, yet, before she had a chance to grab it, the sound of footsteps raced toward her. Suddenly, the door flung open. A man rushed in, slamming the door closed behind him.

5

The first thing Pearl noticed were the bullets of sweat dripping down from the man's temples. He wore a trucker style hat, and he had a bigger build than most. He had a grey t-shirt covering his protruding belly, with a sleeveless, stonewash denim jacket, blue jeans, and worn-down sneakers. He carried a rusty shovel in his hands that was covered in blood, and hanging on his wrist appeared the same bracelet Pearl had hanging on hers: a number of chain links and a single, pink pearl. Pearl backed up into a corner and remained silent, as she stared at him with fear, yet curiosity.

"Who are you?" He asked her, looking at her with the same wariness.

"Pe—Pearl. Who are you?"

"Mike." He turned back to double check that the door had closed securely. Then, looking at Pearl, he asked "What brings you here?"

Pearl looked at him, astounded. "Um, The Maze?"

"No shit," he replied.

Pearl's expression grew puzzled and her patience grew short. She glared at him and raised an eyebrow, and her eyes opened wide. She stated, "You're a seeker, too. You have the same bracelet as me..."

He looked at hers, then back down at his own wrist. "Almost the same. I have a few more chains than you."

Pearl looked down at hers, then back at his. "What are you doing here?" She asked.

"Getting the fuck away from that woman. What's that smell?"

"Shit." Pearl said blatantly.

"Smells like it."

Just then, more footsteps began to pound the floor on the other side of the door. Pearl's shoulders shot up toward her ears, and the man's copied.

"What's happening out there?" Pearl asked him frantically.

"Grab a weapon, anything. Just grab something. Now!" He ordered her. Pearl looked around the bathroom with her heart beating out of her chest. She reached down for the mop, coddled it like a baseball bat, and stared at the door. "We're going to take this bitch down. Get ready." He backed up toward Pearl, preparing to fight.

Pearl had no clue what to do, but she felt more than willing. She stood up tall, pressed her feet firmly into the floor, and prepared for the worst. *What could be worse than what I have already gone through?* She could not even imagine the possibilities.

As the footsteps grew louder from the other side, suddenly, the door-knob jolted, and the door opened wide. From the other side came the wrinkled woman with long, brown hair, yet, this time, her eyes were completely black, and her wrinkled skin appeared to be sunken into her face like a skeleton. She reached her arms out in front of her, let out a ferocious screech, and came after them. Mike took his shovel, pulled it back behind his head, and swung it forward with all his might, swinging it into the woman's skull hard enough to put her down. She collapsed to the floor with blood pouring out of her mouth. Pearl and Mike stood up tall, looking down on the defeated without regret.

"Come on, follow me. Quickly." Mike ran out of the bathroom as Pearl followed like a sheep, hugging the mop's handle close to her.

6

The two of them made their way out from the foul bathroom and back into the eerie hallway. The man led them to the stairs, running back toward the first floor with Pearl following close behind. As they made a run for it, stomping their feet down the timber steps, they were instantly stopped by a young man staring blankly at them from the bottom of the staircase.

The first thing Pearl and Mike noticed about this man was his attire. He had shackles strapped onto his feet and hands, and he wore a prisoner's uniform with black and red stripes. Yet, something about this man appeared off. He had a crazed look in his eye, and the hair on his head stood up like he had been shocked a few dozen times. He had an unnerving smile painted across his face and drool dripping from his chin. Yet, despite his chained wrists, he wore no bracelet. Both seekers' skin crawled, and they stopped halfway down the steps.

"Do you see him, too?" Pearl asked Mike, shaking in her shoes.

"Yeah, I see him," Mike replied under his breath. He lifted the shovel and took a few steps closer to the bottom of the stairs, keeping his eyes locked on the otherworldly man. Pearl followed. "Who are you?" Mike shouted at the shackled man.

The man stared back, releasing an enormous belly laugh. He placed his shackled hands over his stomach and raised his chin up to the sky, guffawing repulsively. Then, he stepped away from the bottom of the steps and made his way into the middle of the room. Mike turned to Pearl, then started to make his way down the stairs, with her following. In front of the burning fireplace, the inhumane prisoner stood hunched, still laughing to himself like he was at a comedy show. Mike looked over his shoulder and glanced at Pearl, nudging his head toward the opposite corner of the room. Pearl picked up the hint and shuffled her feet to the corner, gripping the mop close to her body.

"What are you doing here, man?" Mike asked the laughing man.

He continued laughing to himself, the volume growing louder by the second.

"Yo, man, what the fuck are you doing here?!" Mike asserted.

Still, no response, only laughter. His laughter grew so loud that it began to vibrate the whole room. Mike clenched his eyes shut, and with all his might, he raised the shovel high and swung it like a bat, striking the man across the jaw. The man's head turned almost all the way around, until his laughter came to an immediate halt. Rather than falling to the floor, the crazed man slowly turned his head back in Mike's direction, blood dripping out his mouth, and flashed one more, final smile. Then, within an instant, the prisoner reached his hands around Mike's face, clasped his shackles tight around his neck, and lifted him up off his feet with unbelievable strength, hanging him like a coat on a coat rack.

"Stop!" Pearl screamed from afar.

The prisoner began laughing out loud once again, this time, louder than ever before.

"Let him go!" Pearl screeched. She ran toward him, but by the time she got to them, Mike's flailing feet grew still, and just like that, his life seeped from his body and moved on to his next door. The man dropped Mike like a ragdoll and chuckled at his limp, lifeless body.

Pearl shifted her weight back and forth from each foot. She held onto the mop and stared deeply into the possessed man's eyes. He looked back at her, and his smile only grew wider.

"What do you want?" Pearl asked hesitantly.

He continued to laugh. However, in the midst of his hysteria, silence suddenly swept over him and his manic eyes opened wide. His smile faded into a frown and he grew visibly worried. The man shifted his gaze up at the ceiling. "They're here," he whispered.

Pearl stared at the man, equally as wide-eyed. Fearful, she took a few steps back away from him. "Who's here? What are you talking about?"

He slowly lowered his head, and with tears in his eyes, he said to her, "The masters of my mind."

7

An uneasy feeling swept throughout Pearl and she shook nervously, like a dog at the pound. The hair on her skin shot up high and her heart pounded out of her chest. Suddenly, the sound of voices flooded the room. These voices spoke quietly, at first. They sounded deep, like a man's voice, and they spoke with a deceiving tone, but Pearl could not make out the words. It sounded like pure gibberish. Meanwhile, as a few short moments went by, these senseless voices grew only louder, to the point that they were just about screaming. It was like they spoke through an intercom throughout the room that had been set to full volume.

The man covered his ears and dropped down to his knees. He could not take the screams, for it only drew him more mad. His head began to twitch, shaking back and forth as if he were about to seize. As he did so, the voices racing through Pearl's ear began to morph into a woman's voice, until suddenly, it morphed into her own. The words became clear, and frankly, more than familiar. They screamed "you will never make it out alive," "you aren't strong enough," "you are worthless," and "you are better off dead".

Pearl slapped both hands on each of her ears and muffled the voices away. However, despite her covered ears, the voices seemed to only grow louder. Pearl quickly realized that the voices speaking to her this way were not outside of her, rather, they were the thoughts constructed within her own head. These were the thoughts she submitted to on a daily basis, speaking to her like she was a slave to her own mind. These thoughts spoke so loudly and so mercilessly that the wooden floor began to shake beneath her feet.

Pearl dropped to her knees like the shackled man. They both sat low to the ground, hunched over, while hugging their legs to their chests. They were slaves to their own thoughts. Each of them suffered and succumbed to the lying lips in their minds, giving into the dishonest notions that controlled them constantly. No matter how hard she tried to block out the dark thoughts that raced through one ear and out the other, she could not help but grow only more overwhelmed. "Give up, now." "Why move on?" "You're worthless." "You have no purpose." "The world would be better off if you were dead." Her thoughts lied to her. It was as if she was truly going crazy, so much to the point that her vision began to pixelate before her. She opened her mouth to let out one, miserable scream, and with her next breath in, Pearl collapsed face first onto the wood. The world went black.

# Door #9
# My Dictator is Fear

1

Pearl's eyes opened wide and she gasped for a familiar, deep breath in. Her body shot up and off The Maze floor, like she had just been brutally wakened from a night terror. She sat up straight, light of breath, with her heart racing. As her consciousness regained sight of what was going on, she immediately looked down at the bracelet on her wrist. She counted one less link, leaving only two, individual chain links dangling alongside the pink, shiny pearl. She grasped her wrist with her opposite hand and held it close to her heart, revealing the biggest, most hopeful smile she ever made before.

Her eyes fell heavy for a moment, and she thought to herself, *I am almost there. I can do this.* Her chin tucked closer toward her chest as she recollected her breath. She sat there in silence, however, she remained inside of her screaming mind. It was then that Pearl made another ground-breaking self-discovery. She lifted her head up in a daze, and began to think to herself.

Pearl began listening to her thoughts in a way she had never done before. The thoughts in her head spoke differently this time, or perhaps the true difference was the way Pearl listened. At first, her mind jabbered loudly. Pearl thought about all the time she spent on thoughts that did not serve her. Then, she thought about how deceiving these thoughts could be. She thought about how easily she got caught up in them, and how she let them run her mind wild. *Whoa,* she thought, as she caught herself suffocating on these irrelevant thoughts racing through her mind once again. For the first time, Pearl saw her thoughts as separate from herself. In the last door, Pearl realized her emotions were not a part of her. Like her emotions, she understood her thoughts, too, fooled her mind into attachment. As her thoughts spoke, she tuned into them as if she were listening from a third person point of view. She became fully aware of her thoughts as if they were something other than her own, observing them like they were a train passing her by, or a star shooting high up in the sky. She listened to them travel through the tunnel of her mind, and she heard them for all that they were: simply just thoughts. Pearl realized that she was not her thoughts, and she no longer felt the need to believe she was. Rather than believing the conniving voices inside her head were part of her, she saw them for what they really were: powerless thoughts that only gained mastery when rendered to be true. Thoughts are powerless. It is not unil one attaches emotion to their thoughts, as well as reacts to their thoughts, that the thoughts become powerful. When one identifies with a thought, they become that thought. If one claims, "I am this," "I am that," they manifest it into their life. If one's thoughts are racing through one ear and out the other, they dismiss the present moment. It is more than uncovering the root of one's anxiety, depression, and numbness; it is becoming aware of one's highest Self. The power of the mind is unfathomable, and once one chooses to be the master of their mind rather than the slave, they may access the power to rule their world. Pearl grew an understanding that she had never known existed before, yet this awareness was not all that she came here for. This consciousness was a tool to use for the lessons she would learn next. Or rather, it was another layer of the onion that had peeled back before her; a shed of the skin that hid her truth deep within. With a radiant smile painted from ear to ear, Pearl took a fulfilling deep breath in, and an even deeper breath out. She pierced her eyes down the blood red hallway that stretched long before her, welcoming her further into the gut-wrenching unknown. Without thinking twice, Pearl placed her hands into the floor, pushed herself onto her feet, and set foot toward the second to last door.

She walked with her head high and her guard up. The hair on her skin stood up tall and fear crept through her entire being. Despite every experience she had gone through thus far in The Maze, The Maze itself was a living nightmare. Pearl walked, uneasy, yet determined to make it through. Slowly and with anticipation, she made her way further down the hall, until she faced two different paths leading to two different directions. Pearl paused, taking a moment to perceive each hall and consider what they could possibly lead to. However, just like many halls before, they appeared dark, barely lit, and hard to see through. From the looks of it, they both guided Pearl into unfamiliar territory and further into the dark. Pearl thought for a moment, then realized it did not matter. Whichever way she went, she was destined to go. So, she took a conscious breath in, and turned toward the left, following her gut and hallway down the path to somewhere.

Eventually, the hallway turned around the corner. Pearl craned her head around the corner first, examining the next steps she would endeavor. She observed that this new hall appeared identical to the last, piercing blood red walls with a never-ending ceiling up above. At the end of this oncoming hall, she noticed the hall turn a left corner, curving into oblivion. But despite the path still making its way forward, she noticed that this hallway contained a watertight bulkhead door, one you would find on a naval ship, standing against the left wall. The door was made of metal, it did not stand too tall, and it had a rounded door frame that looked to be bolted into the wall. In the center of the door hung a metal handwheel, screwed down with tight, rusted bolts. The hair on Pearl's arms rose tall as she perceived this entrance. She was interested, but scared to death.

Pearl made her way around the corner and into the new hallway toward the peculiar door. She moved with caution, still holding onto her being with guarded protection, until she finally found herself face-to-face with the door. She lifted her hand away from her body and connected her fingertips to the metal. Her fingers grazed down, wrapping around the handwheel and brushing over the rusted bolts. She absorbed the sensation of the cold, tarnished door with wariness, squinting her eyes to focus even more.

Immediately, the sound of footsteps began echoing from further down the hall, sprinting in her direction with a masculine, screaming voice following."Somebody help me! For God's sake, somebody save me!"

Pearl shot a glance down the hall, waiting to see who would come around the upcoming corner. Her eyes grew wide and her shoulders rose tall. She anticipated the future with fear and could not comprehend what the next few moments had to offer her.

Out from around the corner at the end of the hall, a man came running for his life. Before he could fully turn the corner toward her, the sound of a heavy machine gun blasted through the hall, leaving behind an echo of shock. The man was shot about four times in his back, once in his neck, and twice in his skull. Blood flung out from the front of his body, splattering out onto the wall in front of him. Following the bullets, pieces of his brain flung out of his skull and his body immediately flew forward, smacking into the floor. A pool of blood flooded underneath him, and his insides disemboweled. He was dead instantly.

Pearl grabbed hold of the metal handwheel like a madwoman. She gripped the wheel, using all of her power to turn the wheel open, yet, it would not budge. She kicked her foot up on the door frame and pressed her weight into it, turning the wheel intentionally harder. Sweat dripped down the temples of her face, leaking down off her body. Her eyes, still flooded with tears, had a clear vision, and they would stop at nothing to get there.

As she continued trying to turn the wheel, another pair of footsteps began sprinting down the hall from the same direction the lifeless man had come from. She paused for a moment, looking forward to see what it could be. This time, she heard another voice scream in terror. "Stop! Please stop!" The voice grew louder the closer it became.

Pearl kept her hands clasped on the handwheel, using all her strength to turn it open. Her breath flowed rapid, her heartbeat raced, and a release of adrenaline poured throughout her whole being. The nerves in her body ignited with apprehension and goosebumps speckled all over her body. Her physical being grew hot and her stomach turned in every direction. Within seconds, the sound of running footsteps grew louder toward Pearl. Before she knew it, her life was flashing before her eyes. She felt terrified inside the nightmare she had created herself.

"Fucking open!" She exclaimed to herself, shaking the wheel between her sweaty grip.

The footsteps ran faster toward her, growing louder with every step. Suddenly, the wheel began to budge, moving inch by inch. Pearl took a great inhale and turned the wheel as hard as she could. Finally, the handwheel became loose, spinning all the way around until the metal door cracked open. She pushed the door open as it slowly dragged across the ground. With little time to spare, she cracked it open enough to squeeze her way through to the other side. Pearl quickly closed the door behind her, her breath frantic.

3

The footsteps running grew louder and began to vibrate the path. Pearl, with her chest facing the bulkhead door, pressed her right ear against the metal and listened closely to the other side. Her teeth chattered, while sweat rolled down her face, over her cheek, and dripped off her chin.

The stampeding footsteps raced all the way until they approached the other side of the door. Immediately, the footsteps came to a halt, while the sound of a shrieking voice came to life.

"Please don't! Please spare me! Please!!" The voice of a man, he cried with barbarity. His desperate plea of his dismay shook the whole hall. Pearl could feel his fear, and she too, internally begged for mercy. Then, the sound of a blade leaving a sheath pulsated through the room. Suddenly, the sound of a serrated knife piercing through the body of the screeching man echoed from the other side, leaving behind a resonance of tearing, ripping flesh. She could hear his insides come out of his body, and the shrill sounds of torture made Pearl's skin crawl and her blood freeze over. It was a sound of madness; a wavelength of evil.

The palms of Pearl's hands covered her mouth while her jaw trembled open. The mixture of tears and saliva dripped off her quivering lips and her pupils dilated in terror. She silently sobbed, but she continued to listen.

After about five or six jabs into the helpless body, the insanity paused. Soon, a set of footsteps shuffled their way around outside the door, quickly fading away down the hall. The only thing left to be heard was the thumping of Pearl's beating heart. She felt as if each beat pulsed through her temples, her forehead, and her cheeks. Her stomach bundled tightly in a knot and her whole body shook.

Pearl, with the front of her body still facing the metal door, slowly began to observe her new surroundings. She shifted her gaze over her left shoulder and looked back behind her. Her body followed as she quickly spun around, pressing her back into the door. Her shoulders remained squished against her ears and her tailbone tucked down. From head to toe, Pearl stood stiff, terrified, and uncomfortable in the unknown. She took a deep breath in, yet she held onto her breath out.

4

Pearl found herself standing in a compact hallway made of concrete. The back wall stood about eight feet in front of her, the ceiling about two and a half feet overhead, and the width of the hall stretched about three and a half feet across. She lifted both of her hands and pressed her palms against the walls by her sides. The walls around her were a greyish-white color, with many deep cracks trickling throughout. Each crack in the wall appeared wet, some even with droplets leaking and dripping down. The hall looked as if it were submerged under a thousand feet of water and could be ready to implode any second. Even the pressure Pearl felt within her skull felt heavy, as if she were sitting at the bottom of the deep end of a pool. In the center of the hall hung a single lightbulb off a frayed extension cord. The light flickered every few seconds and it slowly swayed side to side, exposing child-sized footprints faded into the floor below, making their way further down the narrow hall. This area oozed caution and dismay from every corner.

Pearl's ears plugged up and her hair on her skin rose tall. She felt completely consumed with fear from head to toe, but she knew she could not turn back now. She followed the footsteps below her feet.

Pearl made her way forward, moving slowly, wide-eyed, and alert. Her fingertips grazed the walls by her sides, feeling the rugged texture of the cement. She could sense the low vibrational frequency of this room. A chill crawled up her spine and she felt so terrified that she felt physically sick.

As she inched closer toward the end of the hall, she noticed the hallway turn to the right, leading down another path. The imprinted footprints followed, making their way around the corner, too. She paused for a moment, both physically and mentally. Stealthily, she peered around the corner. This hallway led into another short, narrow hall almost identical to the one she stood in, and the footsteps went all the way through to the end. However, at the end of this hall, Pearl could see an opening to the left, one that led to pitch darkness.

Pearl's throat felt as dry as a bone. She could feel her nerves pass through her throat, down her esophagus, and into her stomach. *I've got this, I can do this,* she thought to herself. She shifted her gaze toward the lightless room at the end of the hall, and in that moment, she sensed she was not alone. With apprehension, she continued moving forward.

She moved her body around the corner, still connecting her fingertips to the walls by her sides. Stepping her feet lightly, one after the next, she tiptoed in secrecy. Suddenly, she found herself only a few steps away from the dark room. She stopped for a moment, taking a rich breath in. Fear surfaced at once. Adrenaline overcame her whole being and it was as if time had frozen around her. She felt out of her body, and she felt as though she were walking into a trap. It was then when she realized she was approaching the darkest part of her mind, darker than any part of The Maze so far. She exhaled.

Pearl stepped her feet forward and stood in front of the colorless room. She placed her right hand into the room to guide her first, staying connected to the wall. Her palm grazed the concrete by her side in search for what could be a light switch. She inched forward more, involuntarily holding her breath in her lungs. After a few more steps, her fingertips rubbed over what felt to be a switch. With one finger, she flipped it up.

The first row of lights turned on and shined over the front two corners of the room and everything in between. When they beamed, Pearl noticed a rugged desk made of wood that faced away from the wall. Behind the desk sat a rusty, metal chair with bolts sticking out along its side and spiderwebs intertwined throughout. Hanging on the wall above those two, Pearl noticed a slate chalkboard that looked as if it had not been wiped down in years. An individual piece of yellow chalk sat underneath the board with a soiled, shriveled up felt eraser by its side. She noticed the steps printed into the floor continued their way toward the back corner of the room, further into the dark. Her first thought was that she found herself in an old, outdated classroom.

Then, the second row of lights flickered on slowly after the first. This time, the lights revealed five small elementary school desks lined next to one another. Each desk had a scratched, wooden top and a withered metal chair sitting by its side. The seats appeared empty, but they all carried a lingering sense of the lost souls that had once sat there. Pearl's eyes remained glued on the footprints pursuing further into the darkness.

After, the third row of lights flashed. Just like the set of lights before, they uncovered another five desks sitting next to one another and the footsteps still traveling deeper. Pearl's heart began beating faster out of her chest as she anticipated the remaining lights.

Subsequently, the fourth row of lights flooded with illumination. Five more wooden desks with empty, metal chairs, and imprinted footsteps exposed themselves.

Finally, the last set of lights flickered on and illuminated the back of the room, revealing the room in its entirety. Identical to the others, the last five desks appeared. The back walls were windowless and were covered with sheets of paper with drawings of poorly constructed stick figures drawn by crayon. However, sitting in the last desk in the back corner of the room sat fear itself. The little boy with a thousand daggers in his mouth. His demonic eyes stared deeply at Pearl, piercing her eyes with an evil aura and a wicked smile painted across his face.

Pearl froze in the doorway, staring at the boy like she had just witnessed a ten-car pile up. Her hands hovered nervously in front of her and her whole body shook. She could feel sweat seep from every pore she had, and goosebumps speckled across every inch of her body. At one point, her heart pounded so hard that she believed it would burst out of her chest.

The boy continued to stare at Pearl shaking in her shoes. Slowly, he pushed his chair out from the table and stood up onto his feet. His smile grew wider, almost all the way to his earlobes.

Pearl took a step back, her eyes still locked with the boy's. The boy began to giggle into his boney, bruised hands. His laugh rang loud and it had a scratchy cord to it. Pearl cringed.

"What do you want from me?" Pearl asked the boy, her voice low and steady.

The boy continued to laugh.

"What do you want from me!?" Pearl screeched at the top of her lungs.

He kept laughing. This time, even harder. His laughter quickly became so powerful and full that it vibrated the whole room. It pierced through Pearl's ears like nails on a chalkboard. It sounded almost as though someone were turning up his laugh like a song on the radio. It felt so painful that Pearl's ears were about to bleed. She pressed the palms of her hands into her ears like her head was about to explode.

Out of nowhere, the boy set off on foot, sprinting toward Pearl. He jumped over the desks one after another like a wild animal, all while maintaining the terrifying, soul-feasting smile. Suddenly, the lights shut off and the room flooded with darkness once again.

Without thinking, Pearl instantly spun her body around and ran out of the room. Her feet ran faster than they ever ran before. Her lungs, gasping for peace, inhaled nothing less than panic. Making her way down the hall, she flung her body around the corner making her way back toward the bulkhead door. Meanwhile, the boy's laughter continued to flood the air. When she came around the hall and faced the metal door, she was pleased to find that the door she had come through had not disappeared like every other one she had come through. It remained present and offered Pearl an out.

Pearl gripped her sweaty fingers around the handwheel, turned it forcefully, pulled the heavy door back, and heaved her body through. She pulled it back closed and put her ear close to the door. The laughter stopped immediately.

5

She made it out.

"Ha, ha, ha, ha!" Pearl laughed out loud, relieved, and out of breath.

Amid what she believed to be a victory, she stumbled, accidentally tripping on the bloodbath that sat rotting outside the door from before. She looked down at her feet, and she noticed her right heel sinking into an oozing, dismantled eye socket. There were stab wounds throughout the person's face and all over his torso. It was as if someone continued puncturing him for fun, knowing his life was gone, but just wanted to be *extra* sure.

Pearl screamed and jumped back, slamming herself into the other wall. She stared down at the body, got a quick smell of the rotting corpse, and gagged. She continued to step backwards, far enough to not pay any more attention to the body, yet still close enough to smell the decay. *What next?* She wondered. *I escaped the door unlike any door before. Did I beat The Maze? I couldn't have... Why would I still be here, then?* She looked around, puzzled, until she remembered her bracelet.

Pearl looked down at her wrist and saw nothing but naked skin. The bracelet no longer hung from her wrist, and she immediately grew frantic. She shot a quick glance at her left wrist, back to her right, and then back to the left. *Where could it be?* She thought.

Pearl looked all around her, down by her feet, by the crumbling corpse, and every possible place it could be. Yet, nothing. It was gone.

"No, no, no, this cannot be happening! It's gone!" Pearl's heart began to beat fast and furiously. Her body began growing hot and anxiety churned within her stomach. Losing her bracelet had to be the scariest thing Pearl had seen in The Maze thus far. Her key to escape, her guide to survival, had vanished right before her eyes. The one thing she had to protect the most had disappeared, just like that. She had become stuck in The Maze, just like the rest of the prisoners wandering throughout.

"Oh, fuck," Pearl said to herself. "I'm stuck here." Pearl pressed her back against the red wall, slid down to the ground, and buried her face into her knees. She wept in defeat, and for a split second, she felt just like she did when first had entered The Maze; confused, hopeless, worthless, and timorous.

# FOREVER TRAPPED

1

Pearl sat on the floor of The Maze as if it were the beginning of the end of her life. She wondered how this could have happened, how her bracelet could have left her wrist, and how she had not even noticed. *How did I let this happen? Was there something I could have done differently? Is it too late?* She wondered.

Throughout her clouded thoughts, she found clarity. She slowly peeled her face away from her knees and glared back over toward the metal door. The door stared back at her.

She picked herself up and onto her feet and made her way back to the door with the rotting body guarding it. *Maybe the bracelet fell off on the other side of the door,* she thought to herself. She realized then that she had two choices. She could either stay here, lost in The Maze with nobody to save her, forever wondering how freedom and happiness would feel, or she could go back into the door and face fear itself; the ultimate dictator. Pearl did not come this far to only come this far. She took a deep breath in, and an even greater exhale out. Pearl stepped over the dismantled body, grabbed the metal handwheel, and pushed it open once again, tiptoeing back inside.

2

The door welcomed her back into the narrow, white hallway that looked as if it were about to combust. Just like before, there hung an individual, flickering lightbulb on a single wire, and the walls continued to seep water through the cracks. The only difference she noticed was a second pair of footprints printed into the floor, the same size as the first, making their way around the corner, and back into the darkness.

Pearl gulped, glaring at the other side of the hall. She shifted her gaze down to the floor and hoped to find the bracelet within plain sight. Unfortunately, Pearl knew it would not be that easy.

She made her way through the concrete walls, keeping her eyes glued on the floor in search of her bracelet. She followed both pairs of footprints around the corner, until she made her way closer to the eerie classroom. This time, she noticed the lights appeared turned on. Still not seeing a sign of her bracelet in the hall, she swallowed, took a conscious breath in and out, and crept further toward the classroom.

Pearl crept further to the doorway. Before entering, she peered, expecting the little boy to be exactly where he sat before, but this time, she could not believe her eyes.

"What the fuck?" Pearl said out loud. She stepped into the classroom. Her eyes scanned the room left to right and left again. *What the fuck? Where is he? He was just here.* She thought to herself. *Maybe I can find the bracelet before he returns.*

Pearl made her way through the classroom, trembling as she zigzagged through the desks with her eyes locked on the floor. She dropped to her knees a couple of times, looking under desks and by their sides. She even went to the big desk that sat in the front of the class, yet still no bracelet.

"Where the fuck is it??" Pearl whispered out loud, her heart beating faster and faster. She could feel her body grow more tense as the idea of being trapped in The Maze forever began to set in even more. Her mind began racing. She noticed her monkey mind chatter louder and louder, so much so that she could barely think. So, she took a moment for herself. Pearl sat onto the big, wooden desk, closed her eyes, and took a deep breath in. "Okay Pearl, don't panic. I'm gonna find it. I'm gonna find the bracelet and be home soon. Everything is gonna be okay. Everything is going to work out exactly as it should." Pearl spoke to herself. She exhaled her breath, releasing some anxiety that had trickled through her veins. Suddenly, within the pep talk, and with her eyes still closed, a subtle breeze brushed against her face. Pearl quickly opened her eyes, looked over toward the oncoming breeze, and found herself locking eyes with an open window on the other side of the room.

Pearl scurried to the window, confused yet more than interested. She felt positive that this window was not there before. *There is no way I wouldn't have noticed it, right?* She questioned herself.

The window sat up high on the wall and appeared small and square, just barely big enough for her to climb through. Pearl pulled up a desk, climbed on top, and peeked out the window. On the other side, she noticed a screen of barren birch trees, just like the forest she found herself in the fourth door, where she had sunken into quicksand. However, between two, tall, leafless birch trees, Pearl noticed the little boy with a thousand teeth, standing before her and holding her bracelet in his hand. He wore a devious grin on his face while his eyes pierced deeply through Pearl. He giggled, revealing his rows of teeth, then sprinted into the forest.

"Stop!" Pearl shouted to him. The boy continued racing through the trees, until she could no longer see him.

Pearl pushed herself up, shimmied her body through the window, and jumped out from the other side, landing her feet firmly onto the forest floor. The weather felt cold, just like before. A strong wind blew through the forest, howling through her ears. The air itself felt eerie, and she could not tell if her hair stood up and off her skin from the chilling tempera-ture outside, or from the fear that lingered throughout her veins. *Probably both,* she considered. She squinted her eyes and scanned the woodland before her. No sign of the boy.

Pearl started running into the depths of the forest. She ran past the trees, dodging branches and jumping over every obstacle in her way. Her heart pulsed almost as fast as her feet ran, and despite the cool air, sweat dripped down her face.

After a while of running, Pearl slowed back down, then finally came to a halt. She stood there, in the middle of vastness, a vastness that appeared so massive and endless that it felt too overwhelming to even think about.

"Where the fuck did you go, you little monster?" She spoke under her breath. The boy was nowhere to be found. Pearl found herself scanning the forest again, focusing on anything that caught her eye. The only thing moving before her were the fallen leaves along the forest floor, dancing within the subtle, chilled breeze. She gritted her teeth, and her breath grew short once again.

3

After spending hours on top of hours searching for the demonic boy, the day quickly turned into the night. The sun began to set, leaving behind a beautiful hue of yellow, orange, pink, and purple illuminating the sky. Pearl looked up, admiring the rainbow above. As the sky began to alter, the temperature followed. The once chilled breeze morphed into practically freezing. Goosebumps speckled over every inch of Pearl's body, even underneath her clothes, and with every exhale, she could see her breath leave her lips. Before she knew it, the sun had fully dismissed itself, welcoming another full moon. Through the dorment branches, the moon cast a white light that shone over the forest, just enough to lead Pearl's way. *What am I going to do?* Pearl thought to herself, quickly losing hope. Pearl scanned the forest once again, squinting her eyes to get a better look. She knew that searching for the boy at night would not get her far, so she decided to seek shelter and warmth.

Pearl sauntered through the forest, so much so that she found herself at the foot of a large mountain. She continued to follow the mountain face, until she suddenly stumbled across a large opening to a cave tucked away into its side. Pearl stopped for a moment, freezing over as she exhaled into the palms of her hands. She glanced over her shoulder, perceiving nothing more than white, barren birch trees illuminating underneath the moonlight. She looked forward once again, making her way to the cave's mouth.

Before she entered, she stared in from the outside. The cave was darker than dark, wet, and chilling. It was quiet, for the only thing Pearl heard from the inside was a slow, repetitive dripping noise that came from deeper within. Despite the cave's unsettling nature, it provided more warmth than the outside did. Pearl tiptoed inside and huddled against the cave's wall, close enough to the opening to see the forest around her, yet far enough inside to keep her slightly warmer. She rested her back against the cave, placed her hands on her growling stomach, and let out an exhausted exhale.

Pearl's mind began racing once again, yet her awareness of her thoughts made them easier to listen to. She wondered if she would find the little boy, or if the little boy would find her. She wondered if she would ever make it out of The Maze, or if she would become a prisoner for the rest of eternity. She couldn't fathom what it would be like to live here forever, yet this glimpse of what could be left her stomach turning even more. After a few more hours of submitting to fear, questioning herself and her situation, she remembered that no matter how much time she spent on unnecessary thoughts, she knew it would not change a thing. At that very moment, the situation was out of her control, and focusing on unserving thoughts would do more harm than good. The only thing Pearl needed to do was relax until morning. Eventually, she managed to rest her eyes just enough to get only a couple hours of restless sleep, just in time for the sun to barely rise once again.

## 4

*Tap, tap, tap.* A finger poked Pearl's shoulder. Like she had a fire under her ass, Pearl awoke abruptly, jumped up onto her feet, and flew back in disbelief. The little boy stood in front of her, looking up at her with an even more cunning grin. Pearl stared down at him with pure terror in her eyes. Her lips quivered heavily and she trembled in her shoes.

"Hi," she murmured.

The boy said nothing back. Instead, he kept his shrewd smile. Pearl looked down at his hands and noticed her dangling bracelet between his grimy, lifeless fingers.

"Ca—can I have my bracelet back, please?" She asked ever so politely.

The boy began laughing, not with her, but at her.

Pearl's body became covered in goosebumps. The sound of his laugh was so hair raising, that she felt like crawling out of her own skin. "Please, I need it back," she begged, disturbed, terrified, and desperate.

"Why do you want it back?" He asked her, his voice shrewd and devious as he began making his way out of the cave, back into the barren forest.

"Because I need it. I need that bracelet back." Pearl followed him.

The boy stopped in his tracks. He pulled the bracelet behind his back, hiding it from Pearl. "But, don't you want to stay here with me forever and ever?"

Pearl felt her heart sinking deep into her stomach. The thought of staying here forever made her want to hurl. A tear began to shed from her eye, yet she held her strength. "No, I don't want to stay here. I want to go back home."

"But what about all the games we could play together?" The boy began skipping in circles, jumping up and down as he flailed his arms in the air like any other excited, little kid.

Pearl opened her mouth and began to speak. "I don't want—" Suddenly, her voice grew inaudible. She began to recollect her thoughts, thinking back on every other door she had been through and the lessons she had learned so far. She remembered the girl with the pierced nose, who, although heavily intoxicated, spoke words of wisdom. She considered what she had told herself about how every seeker had a chaser, and how it all was just an illusion. Pearl's worried eyes grew angry. She began stepping back without even thinking.

"You're not real. Nothing about you is real," she talked down to the boy.

The boy's jumping body became stiff as he stared back at Pearl. His slithering smile slowly morphed into an unnerving scowl.

"You're an illusion." Pearl accused him, while pointing at her temple. "I created you. You're just a figment of my fucking imagination."

"You don't think I'm real?" The boy asked innocently.

"You aren't real." Pearl pierced her eyes through the little boy and her voice grew more serious. "You aren't anything." For the first time ever, Pearl stood strong, facing fear itself.

5

The little boy's face froze. He stared blankly up at Pearl, as if his mind were racing with his own thoughts and he were lost in a daze. He had a glaze shimmer over his goat like eyes and he stood still like a statue. It was like his consciousness had faded from within him. Pearl raised an eyebrow. *What is wrong with you?* She stuck out her hand in front of his face and waved.

"Hello?"

No response. Not even a flinch.

*I wonder if...* she thought to herself. Instinctively, Pearl reached down to her bracelet that stayed locked away in his hand behind his back. However, just before she grabbed hold of it, the boy's other hand shot up and gripped Pearl's wrist, squeezing her so tight that she thought he would break her.

"Stop! Let me go!" Pearl yelled.

He remained still yet his hand gripped tighter.

"Please!" She begged.

"You think I'm not real," the boy mentioned calmly as if nothing was wrong. "But if I'm not real, how can I do this to you?" He squeezed even tighter. Her hand began turning purple and the pain grew numb.

Suddenly, the little boy started to morph into a not-so-little boy anymore. His spine began growing, stretching him up to about ten feet tall. His face grew long and narrow, and his lifeless skin sunk deeper in its place, exposing nearly every bone in his body. His hands began morphing into claws, while his fingers stretched long like needles. He smiled down on her, revealing his teeth that appeared to be growing longer and sharper. He smiled so big that the corner of his mouth reached all the way up to his temples, and his goat-like eyes began dripping blood from their sockets. The little boy that once haunted her throughout The Maze had transformed into a colossal skeleton who hungered for her flesh, right before her eyes. Pearl's jaw dropped as she gazed up with dismay.

"Do I seem real to you, now?" He asked Pearl with a new, trans-formed voice that spoke deep and rough. Right then, the demonic creature opened his left hand wide and struck the side of Pearl's body, throwing her into one of the birch trees that stood behind her. She flew off her feet, striking the tree so hard that the wind knocked out of her body. She lied on the forest floor hopelessly, looking up at the sky with a tear dripping from her eye. *This is it,* she thought to herself. *This is the end of me.*

6

Pearl lied weakly on the forest floor, taking back her stolen breath. Slowly, she peeled herself off the fallen leaves. Her eyes became clear once again, as she scanned the forest before her. However, the not so little boy no longer stood before her. *Where did he go?* She thought to herself. Meanwhile, his laughter began to echo the forest.

Pearl pushed herself back up to her feet. She turned in circles, looking up and down and all around. Her blood began to boil, and she could feel smoke leaking through her ears. From afar, she noticed a large branch that had broken off from one of the trees. She hobbled over to the branch, picked it up off the earth floor, and prepared for the fight she had been waiting for.

"Show yourself you fucking coward! I'm not scared of you! You mean nothing to me!" Pearl shouted at the top of her lungs, clenching the stick between her hands like a baseball bat.

The laughter grew louder, and the wind blew even harder.

"Fight me! Kill me, I fucking dare you! Show yourself, you piece of shit!"

From behind, the boy's claw made its way through Pearl's hair. He gripped her locks and pulled her so hard that her scalp felt like it was ripping from her skull. Immediately, she turned around, and swung the branch at his skeleton-like hands. She hit him, *hard.* He released his grip, but only for a moment.

The creature ripped the branch from Pearl's hand and swung it back at her like a bat, throwing Pearl into another tree once again. Short of breath and brittle to the bone, Pearl continued to fight. She pushed herself away from the tree and faced the ten-foot boy once again.

"Is that all you got?" Pearl mocked him despite her shortness of breath. Suddenly, Pearl's mind thought of something she had never thought of before. *If I'm back in the forest, that means...* Her eyes opened wide. She had a great idea.

Pearl began limping as fast as she could, making her way deeper into the forest. She continued yelling at the top of her lungs, tormenting the boy.

"Come and get me you fucking coward!" Pearl staggered rapidly through the trees, dodging almost every branch in her way. She kept her eyes wide open in hopes to find what it was she was looking for.

The forest floor underneath her vibrated loudly as the immortal, ten-foot creature chased after her, stomping his massive feet behind. He was so big, so powerful, that the birch trees did not stand a chance. Everything standing in his way came down, yet his evil eyes stayed glued on his prize.

Pearl's feet kept rapid. She lumbered deeper and deeper into the forest, until suddenly, her eye caught a familiar scene. From afar, she noticed the dirt trail once again, and she saw the same hill. Cunningly, she knew her destination was near. The monster continued chasing her, not far behind, as his laughter continued growing even louder.

Pearl continued hobbling as fast as she could, until suddenly, her previous fate became clear. On the ground before her sat the pool of quicksand that had sucked her down before. She stopped in her tracks, right beside the sand, and turned around to face the beast.

"Come and get me!" Pearl screeched confidently, hoping he would fall into the trap like she had.

The creature began to run faster in her direction, first on two feet, until suddenly, he dropped down to all fours, sprinting like a wild animal. He screeched so loudly that Pearl felt as if blood were dripping from her ears.

The demon pounced onto Pearl like a leopard onto a gazelle. He pinned her down into the ground, right beside the pool of quicksand, lodging her skull into the dirt so hard that the world began to spin. He threw her bracelet off to the side, wrapped both of his talon-like hands around Pearl's neck, and began to squeeze the life out of her. His bloody goat eyes stared down at her and he grinned wider with every breath she could not take.

"You know, if you die without your bracelet, you will be trapped here forever. You'll wake up as a prisoner back in The Maze, forever suffering for the rest of eternity, with me, and every other demoralized soul that deteriorates here. How does that sound, Pearl?" He squeezed her neck even harder.

Pearl began choking and her vision began to grow fuzzy.

"Sleep, you weak-minded fool. And forever wake up back in The Maze. This is your home now."

Pearl gasped for breath. She reached her hands up to his, but his arms stretched so long, she could not reach him. Her body squirmed underneath his, until she slowly grew still. With one more desperate attempt for breath, everything began slowly morphing to black.

Suddenly, from afar, a mighty roar echoed the forest. The ten-foot creature looked up in the direction of the growl, until his goat eyes caught sight of the massive, seething grizzly bear she had met five doors before.

7

The monster released his grip and stood back onto his feet.

"What the fuck do you want?" He yelled at the bear.

The bear stared at him like he had been starving his entire life. The bear roared again, shaking the whole forest. Meanwhile, Pearl lied on the floor, barely coherent, trying to catch her breath before the last of it squeezed out of her.

The creature turned to the bear, eager for a fight. He swung both of his long arms up in the air and released a blood-curdling scream.

The bear roared back, this time even louder. The bear stood up onto his back legs, for a moment, howling with the wind. At full height, he was eye to eye with the monster. On the other hand, the morphed boy projected no fear. He continued to scream at the bear, when suddenly, his jaw detached, like a snake when feeding, exposing his teeth even more. He laughed again, and the wind carried the evil tone through the air. Without warning, the boy dropped back down to his hands and feet and made a run for it, charging at the grizzly. The grizzly dropped down to all fours and charged right back, running head-on.

The Earth's floor rumbled underneath Pearl's body, still on the ground. She caught her breath, filling her lungs up once again. Blinking a few times, she tried to focus her vision. Slowly, everything became clear. She stared blankly at the sky above her, noting the naked branches that hung overhead like a canopy. As her back vibrated against the dirt, she turned her head, slowly and weakly, and saw the demon running quickly away from her and toward the bear. Pearl took another shocking breath in, peeling her skull up and off the dirt. She choked on her life force, coughed harshly as she sat up, while her head pounded from within. She felt incredibly feeble, yet tremendously alleviated.

From afar, she witnessed the fight go down. The boy ran as fast as a cheetah, roaring ferociously back at the hungry grizzly. The grizzly ran down the hill, busting through birches like a wrecking ball, bellowing back at him. These quick seconds of anticipation felt like hours to Pearl. She kept her eyes glued on the two beasts and did not blink once.

The bear jumped down, quaking the earth below. He set foot, stampeding his way toward the boy with saliva flinging from his hungry lips. The ten-foot boy screeched one more time at the top of his lungs, until suddenly, he pounced up and off the ground, and onto the grizzly. He pierced his immortal hand through the bear's pelt, sliced open his meat, and poured blood. The bear roared mercilessly, standing back onto his hind legs. The boy jumped off the bear and back onto the dirt, copying the bear's movements. He stood up onto his two legs, too, face-to-face with the bear. Pearl remained seated, still recollecting her breath, as she watched the battle to the death.

Within an instant, the bear clasped his powerful jaw around the boy's scrawny collar bone, digging his teeth into his flesh and puncturing his ghostly skin. The bear released his bite, then chomped again, this time on his neck. The boy screeched, his cry rattling the whole forest. He placed his hands onto the bears chest and shoved him off. The boy then jumped onto the grizzly, wrapping his legs around his head, opened his mouth wide, and bit into the bear's flesh. The bear dropped back onto all fours and whiplashed his body side to side, smashing the boy into the birch trees, breaking through each one. The boy then released his teeth, flew off the bear's neck, and came crashing to the ground. Winded, the boy lied on his back. The grizzly sauntered over to the boy, looked him dead in his bloody goat eyes, and with zero remorse, he opened his mouth wide, and latched onto the boy's skull. Within a single chomp, the boy's screams fell silent, and the wind slowed to a breeze.

8

Pearl's jaw fell heavy as she gawked in disbelief. Instantly, the victorious bear turned his head to Pearl, staring back at her with blood dripping from his lips. The bear stepped off his dinner and made his way through the trees toward Pearl. Pearl remained still, breathing short, uneasy breaths. The anticipation killed her.

He made his way closer. Suddenly, the bear stopped in his tracks, about ten feet from Pearl, and stared deeply into her eyes. Pearl remained still, silent, and strained, hoping he would spare her. Her heart just about fell out of her chest, she felt so afraid.

The bear huffed at her. Then, he looked down at his side and lowered his nose toward the bushes of fallen leaves. *What is he doing? What is he going to do?* Pearl thought to herself.

Slowly, the bear lifted his head once again, looked at Pearl, with her bracelet hanging from his mouth.

Pearl's eyebrows furrowed together. Her breath became faster and her skin crawled even more. She kept in her place, returning the look back to the furry beast. Yet, ever so calmly, the bear made his way over to Pearl. When he reached her, he nodded his head, released the bracelet from his bloody mouth, gave Pearl one last look in the eyes, then turned away. Pearl watched the bear wander back into the forest, alone and unphased.

The bear had disappeared. Quickly, Pearl grabbed ahold of the bracelet. She shifted her gaze down, squeezed the bracelet tightly in her fist, and brought it to her heart. For a moment, she sobbed tears of joy. Rather than running from her fear, she had faced fear. She closed her eyes, took a deep, relieving breath in, and exhaled greatness.

# Her Rude Awakening

1

Pearl opened her eyes once again and found herself standing tall within the blood-red halls of The Maze. As her vision slowly grew clearer, she looked in every direction, taking in The Maze's ambience for the tenth time. She shifted her gaze down, and noticed her fists still pressed into her heart. She opened her hands wide out in front of her, and found her bracelet with a single chain link, followed by the glistening, pink pearl, sitting in the palms of her hands.

"YES!" Pearl shouted out loud. "I did it! I made it out! I'm back!" Pearl tied her bracelet back onto her wrist and smiled greatly. Gratitude swept over her. She let out a chuckle of delight, a sigh of relief, and her eyes burned with joyful tears, knowing that the end of The Maze was near. Pearl took a deep breath in, and an even deeper breath out. However, this ego death came differently than the others. She had no overpowering phenomenon of understanding. Instead, she simply just knew. She had learned the most important lesson of The Maze.

Fear is an illusion that only exists when fed by one's thoughts, one's emotions, and one's actions. As humans, temporarily living a physical existence in a skin vessel, experiencing fear is natural, however, living in fear is not. An emotion that dictates the lives of many, fear is the limiting belief that one creates within their own mind that manipulates their perception about themselves, the world, and life itself. When fear floods the mind and body, one sets limits on themselves that keep them from reaching their fullest potential and from stepping into their highest power. Fear requires a person's thoughts to have more attention than the present moment, so much so that they submit their control to the deceiving dictator, ultimately stepping down into the seat of the slave. It is the root of depression and darkness in the overgrowing garden of one's mind. Living in fear is living in a false reality; it is the made-up story one tells themselves to fulfil their need to remain comfortable, all the while controlling every aspect of their life. Living in fear is not a service to oneself, nor is it a service to Source. For the first time in Pearl's life, instead of running from fear, she faced it. Although Pearl did not physically beat the boy with a thousand teeth, she challenged him head on, and she defended her power with every ounce of her worth. She had realized that living in fear did not serve her, in fact, the power fear had was only as strong as the eye of the beholder permitted it to be. Throughout Pearl's journey through The Maze, before and after hypnosis, she had been running from fear, with fear, because of fear. The little boy with a thousand teeth followed Pearl throughout the outskirts of her mind, when really, he was just a fragment of her psyche that haunted her daily. Every day she lived, she spent living in fear, constantly talking down on herself, constantly limiting herself, and constantly keeping herself captive in the dark. Yet, within this door, Pearl saw fear for what it really was; a limitation. A state of disconnect from Self and Source. *Fear* is a conniving devil that is unworthy of one's pure energy. In that moment, Pearl made the conscious decision to take back her power, dismissing fear from the throne. Now, she was in control.

Pearl continued to stare down at the bracelet, smiling ear to ear as she recounted the single chain again and again. Pearl had come so far that the only thing she had left to do was to fully wake up. She took a conscious, deep breath in through her nose and out through her mouth, and set out toward the tenth door of The Maze.

2

Pearl made her way through The Maze for what she hoped to be the final time. As she walked through the blood red halls, she felt more at ease within herself than she ever had before. She felt lighter on her feet, while the feeling of fear no longer dictated her mind.

Up ahead, she noticed the hall stretch long before her, eventually turning a corner to the left. She followed, with little to no questions.

As Pearl turned the corner, the red on the walls began to fade to pink, to light pink, and then finally, to white. Pearl stopped in the middle of the hall. She looked around at the walls by her side, examining them closely with curiosity and interest. She noticed the cracks that had been splitting through the cement had faded away, too. *What the heck?* She thought to herself. *I've never seen the walls do that before.* She shifted her gaze up toward the never-ending ceiling. Yet, she was surprised to find herself staring at a white ceiling with bright can lights about seven feet overhead. Even the temperature rose from a crisp chill to a comfortable degree, and the lingering smell of decay began fading away. *What's going on right now?* Pearl wondered, holding on to her breath.

Pearl lowered her head back down in the direction of her path and found herself staring at a beautiful, hand-crafted, white, wooden door, glistening at the end of the hallway. *The last door,* Pearl thought to herself. She shifted her gaze down to her bracelet, taking in the presence of the last, single chain and the single pearl hanging from her wrist. She took a conscious breath in and a conscious breath out while making her way closer to the door.

She stepped up to the door, observing all four corners and the crafts-manship in between. She grabbed hold of the knob, and before she turned it, she glanced over her left shoulder one last time, only to find nothing had changed behind her. So, she squeezed her eyes closed, gritted her teeth tight, and turned the knob with anticipation. With little to no effort, it swayed open.

## 3

She stood with her nervous heart sinking into her stomach. Slowly, she blinked her eyes open. On the other side of the door, she saw a single, barren, white-walled room that was lit up bright. Everything inside appeared untouched. The floors below her were made of white marble, and the ceiling above her rose high and shined pure. The four walls within illuminated a naked brightness, and in the middle of the room stood a tall, full-body mirror with a white, metal frame, all by its lonesome. Pearl raised an eyebrow as she crept inside.

The air inside this room felt so good and fresh, it was as if she were breathing beneath a forest created of a million lush trees. She took another breath in, filling her lungs up with this purifying oxygen. It felt so good to stand in this room, that it felt almost uncomfortable. *Is this a trick?* Pearl wondered, for this was unlike anything she had experienced in The Maze. Despite her curiosity, Pearl kept her guard up, and faltered toward the standing mirror.

She approached the mirror with her gaze shifted down toward the marble floor. Before she looked up, she swallowed a dry gulp, took another cleansing breath in, then ever so slowly, looked into the mirror. She began with the reflection of her feet first, until she slowly crawled her vision up her body, all the way up until her eyes locked with the ones in the mirror.

## 4

She saw herself on the outside first. Her hair was a wreck, her face was a mess, and she appeared tired beyond belief. She had a tear in her top, a rip in her jeans, and other parts of her clothes were falling from the seams. Yet, as she stood there, staring at her reflection, her perspective began to shift. Wide-eyed and mesmerized, the woman in the mirror stared back. Their spines lengthened, their shoulders rolled down their backs, their arms rested by their sides, and the crown of their heads reached up toward the ceiling. They both stood there, gazing back at one another.

Suddenly, while Pearl remained as still as a statue, not moving a single muscle, the reflection's hand began to rise, reaching out to Pearl with its fingers spread out wide. Instantly, Pearl's body flashed hot and bullets of sweat seeped from her pores. Pearl's eyes opened wide as she stared, mesmerized at the palm of her reflection's hand. She pierced the mirror with focus, while she followed the hand's movements that moved only on the other side. Pearl's gaze moved away from the hand and traveled up her reflection's body. But, when she looked up at her reflecting face, she noticed that the eyes in the mirror never left the eyes of Pearl, in fact, they had been staring at her the whole time. While Pearl found herself focused on the reflection's hand, the eyes in the mirror did not move once. They had remained locked on Pearl, and only Pearl.

Pearl jumped back and away from the mirror. "What is this?" She spoke aloud, cringing. Meanwhile, her reflection maintained its stance, one hand out to Pearl as if it were giving her a high five. It's eyes remained glued to hers.

Pearl stepped closer to the mirror once again. She rooted both feet down into the floor, lifted her chest up slightly, and balled her hands up into fists, facing her reflection like she faced the boy with a thousand teeth.

Gradually, the reflection brought its other hand to meet its right. Suddenly, with both palms out wide, the reflection reached for its right index finger. With its right hand still flexed back toward its face, the reflection pinched its cuticle and slowly began to peel the skin back, all the way down its finger, all the way to the knuckle.

Pearl covered her mouth and gasped for a breath; her body immediately flooded with terror. However, with her new set of lenses, she knew the only way to let the fear go was to fully step into the discomfort, face the fear, then let it go, just like every other lesson she had learned in The

Maze. So, with tears filling her eyes, she continued to watch her reflection peel back her layers.

It continued to pull the layer of skin back and down its hand, down to its wrist, all the way until the skin snapped off from her body. The fresh, open wound began to deluge blood, dripping down onto the white floor below. Suddenly, her reflection reached both hands up to the sides of its face. A smile slithered across the reflection's face, until suddenly, it gripped its cheeks with its fingernails and deep into the skin. Pearl remained frozen, hypnotized by the sight.

The nails clawed her reflection's face like a cat on a scratching post. It tore through its cheeks, its chin, its nose, and its forehead, ripping pieces of its own face off. The deeper the nails dug, the more blood began to pour. It continued gouging its own face, ripping apart its skin, tissue, and flesh. After its face appeared nothing less than demolished and with little to no skin left, its hands made its way into the hair on its head, ripping every strand from the seams until it had no hair left at all. Pearl screamed out loud, her trembling hands still covering her mouth. Her eyes, hypnotized and drowning in tears, continued to watch her reflection.

Her bloody reflection stopped for a moment. It lowered its hands down by its sides and stared deeply into Pearl's eyes. Pearl stared back, anticipating the reflection's next move. As her reflection returned the look, its eyes glistened at Pearl's, still smiling from ear to ear. Then, it reached for its blood-covered clothes, ripped off its top, removed its shoes, shed its pants, and its underwear, revealing its bare, naked body to Pearl. Pearl remained still, fully clothed and with not one drop of blood. Her hands kept over her mouth and her eyes continued flooding with tears.

Slowly, her reflection rubbed its hands down onto its shoulders, its triceps, its chest, and everything in between, smearing its bloody hands all over its body. It dug its nails deep into its skin, ripping every inch of itself apart. It tore through its very own flesh, shedding its skin like a snake, ripping through tendons, and breaking through muscle. Pearl continued to watch, untouched on the outside, yet slowly dismantling on the inside.

Although she stood with her skin still hugging her body tight, she felt every piece of flesh rip off her reflection, as if she were truly physically dismantling herself. She could feel every tear, every shred, and every rip her reflection made. The sensation felt more than excruciating, so much so that she believed the pain could kill her. Pearl screamed, she cried, she shook, and she felt, yet she could not look away.

As her reflection ripped deeper into its body, it slowly began to expose its intestines and innards for Pearl to see. It worked its hands all the way down its body, past its stomach, hips, and legs, all the way down to the tips of its toes. One layer after another after another, it peeled itself apart, delayering every part of its being, until it had nothing left to rid. *Maybe there was no escaping The Maze,* Pearl thought for a moment, as she stared wide-eyed at the bloody woman in the mirror. Suddenly, amidst the ego death, her reflection transformed into a bright, transparent silhouette, with nothing but a single, shining pearl hovering at its heart space. Within Pearl's next breath, she grew overwhelmed with a sensation of light. Her third eye opened wide.

5

What appeared to be a slow, brutal suicide, concluded to be a profound discovery of Self. As Pearl stood there, facing her silhouette and the pearl hovering on its chest, she uncovered her ultimate truth. Her reflection, who dismantled its physical body, was really peeling back the layers that had built up over her for years. It became clear to Pearl that the layers of her reflection's skin were really the layers of her own onion, layers that were constructed of nothing less than ego, trauma, and tribulation. As these layers piled up, growing on top of one another over time, they covered her beautiful, pink, shiny pearl, so much so that its light grew hidden, until it barely had any light left to shine. Like the pearl, her soul, too, was beautiful, shined bright, and carried an infinite amount of value. These layers covered her pearl—her light, her soul—ultimately disconnecting her from her authentic Self. Over time, the weight of these layers grew heavy, covering her light so much so that darkness overruled her. Every thought, every action, and overall, her everyday reality became captive to the dark. For years, Pearl told herself a story, brainwashing herself without even knowing it. Every trauma, every shadow, and every whisper from the deceiving lips of her thoughts, distracted her from what was truly real. In the physical realm, Pearl unintentionally dragged herself down into The Maze. For years after, she spent her time looking for her way out, yet her light was so dimmed, so could barely find her way. Yet, as she stood captive with the delayered silhouette reflecting in the mirror, captive with the essence of beauty the pink pearl portrayed, she felt the heavy veil lift from her once-sleeping eyes. This process of delayering represented the process of one's awakening journey. An awakening to one's Self, a new, profound connection to one's Self, and an overwhelming sense of power. It was within this moment, Pearl was truly able to let go of everything she had been holding on to, by truly shedding her layers. The fog that clouded her vision faded away, revealing all that was true; happiness, freedom, self-worth, and faith.

One would think that becoming aware of their Self is a sublime, peaceful process that is full of magic, fairies, and butterflies. Well, one could only wish it were that fucking easy. The truth is the awakening process is nothing more than ugly, horrifying, and gut-wrenching. Becoming aware of yourself as you are, a spiritual being temporarily living in a human body, is a crazy, wild, emotional ride.

Before, Pearl lived cluelessly, naïvely, and detached from her Self. She sat as an oblivious speck on the pendulum of life. She believed she was alone and trapped in the deepest, darkest hole of her mind. She believed the darkness to be so dark at times that sometimes, she simply could not breathe, and it was as if the world hungered for her soul. She felt anxious every moment of her life yet numb to the pain. She convinced herself that she was mentally sick, a slave to her own mind, and a slave to fear. Yet, within this door, her awakening journey had commenced.

The awakening process is a journey to self-discovery. When one steps foot on their journey to truth, they make the decision to unlock their ultimate power, by peeling back their layers, deprogramming their mind, and ultimately, connecting back to the Divinity within them and outside of them. During one's awakening, they become aware of their Self, continuously unfolding the parts of themselves they had no idea they had within, removing layers from their ego, and constantly shedding until the day they ascend. They begin to see themselves and the world around them from a different perspective, slowly discovering that nothing outside of them will ever fulfill them. Happiness comes from the inside, and once one realizes that they are the master of their human experience and that they have ultimate control over every thought, every action, and every attitude they hold within themselves, they can consciously choose to use their power to create the reality they want to live. They step into their fullest power, uncovering their light to only reveal a pink pearl shining deep within. They see the truth: The truth of life, the truth of their existence, and the truth of their infinite power within. It takes true courage to look at one's Self, and despite how hard it may be, the reward is ever-lasting.

Pearl stood there, releasing every emotion that surfaced. She cried, she laughed, she grew furious, and she felt joy. She stood hunched, letting go of everything that no longer served her. All of her traumas, all of her emotions, and everything else that did not serve her any longer. As she did so, she noticed the pearl hovering in her heart space began to shine brighter, creating a ball of light that slowly began to flood all throughout her body.

Pearl watched the light grow within her, until she suddenly felt a sensation of powerful relief engulf her whole being. She felt the shackles of her mind detach, and she experienced a sense of freedom like never before. She let go off the thoughts, the beliefs, and the constant judgment of herself. Within this moment, she became the master of her own life. Amidst the tears of trauma and joy, the light flooded her body. Pearl graciously smiled as she wiped her tears from her face. She placed her hands over her heart, closed her eyes, took a deep breath in and out, as she thought to herself, *it was all worth it.*

The world went white.

# PSYCH WARD

1

Tom sat back into his seat with disbelief. For a moment, the room went silent as they all held space with one another, digesting the gruesome tale Doc had told them. Tom looked over his shoulder toward Allan and Randy, then back at Doc. Meanwhile, Doc smiled, proudly leaned back, and placed both hands behind his head.

"Wow, Doctor. That is quite a story," Tom stated.

"I have a lot of great stories! You want to hear another?" Doc exclaimed.

"Maybe another time," Tom responded. "So, back to Pearl. Would you say she reached enlightenment?"

Doc furrowed his brows, leaned forward on the edge of his bed, and let out a chuckle. "Enlightenment is not a destination. It is a journey," Doc responded confidentially, as if Tom should have known the answer already.

"Do you know if Pearl ever escaped The Maze?" Tom asked, looking past Doc's eyes, but close enough to see them looking back at his.

"I'm not too sure, to be honest with you," Doc murmured.

Tom continued. "So, you don't know if she is still trapped in The Maze?"

"No, I don't."

"Then how do you know about all the others that are still trapped there to this day?"

"The people in The Maze today are people that couldn't survive their

273

own shadows. I know Pearl made it to her last door, a door not many people make it to. Only a few have made it to the end, but if they get through it, I really don't know where they go. Maybe they wake up and return to the physical world, or maybe if they are lucky, they'll die and ascend. It will always be a mystery, to me," Doc explained, keeping his voice low and steady.

Tom looked over his shoulder once again, flashing a glance to Allan and Randy. The two of them nodded at Tom, then went about their dues. Tom turned his head slowly back ahead.

"What if I told you, it does not have to be a mystery any longer?" Tom asked.

Doc fell silent, as did the rest of the room. Tom stood up and out of his chair, walked toward the room's entry, and grabbed hold of the knob. Yet, before he opened the door, he looked back at Doc and cracked a small, cunning smile. Then, he opened the door. Standing on the other side, stood the mystery. Pearl's eyes twinkled at Doc and a smile slithered across her face. She made her way into the room, pulled up a chair, and looked Doc straight into his eyes.

"Remember me?" She smiled as she twirled the pink pearl hanging alone on her wrist.

Emerging author Alexandra Russell, has always known her mission here on Earth would involve helping others. Her deep fascination with spirituality, a bizarre interest in horror & thriller genres, and a passion for writing has compelled her to become an author.

After years of battling health issues, fighting depression of her own, and finding her truth within, she knew she had to guide others to do the same.

Before embarking on her writing journey, Alex faced many challenges that pushed her into becoming the woman she is today. She became a certified yoga instructor and received her Business in Entrepreneurship associates degree, then, she turned her attention to assisting those in need.

This is her first novel, but not her last.

Alexandra resides in Southern California.

For more information on Alexandra Russell and her books, visit her website at alexandrarussell.com.